Dave Stone

Keeping Your Head

ABOVE

water

Refreshing Insights for Church Leadership

Flagship church resources
from Group Publishing

Flagship church resources

from Group Publishing

Innovations From Leading Churches

Flagship Church Resources are your shortcut to innovative and effective leadership ideas. You'll find ideas for every area of church leadership including pastoral ministry, adult ministry, youth ministry, and children's ministry.

Flagship Church Resources are created by the leaders of thriving, dynamic, and trend-setting churches around the country. These nationally recognized teaching churches host regional leadership conferences and are respected by other pastors and church leaders because their approaches to ministry are so effective. These flagship church resources reveal the proven ideas, programs, and principles that these churches have put into practice.

Flagship Church Resources currently available:

- *Doing Life With God*
- *Doing Life With God 2*
- *The Visual Edge:*
  Compelling Video Connectors for Your Worship Experience
- *Mission-Driven Worship:*
  Helping Your Changing Church Celebrate God
- *An Unstoppable Force:*
  Daring to Become the Church God Had in Mind
- *A Follower's Life:*
  12 Group Studies on What It Means to Walk With Jesus
- *Leadership Essentials for Children's Ministry*
- *Keeping Your Head Above Water:*
  Refreshing Insights for Church Leadership
- *Seeing Beyond Church Walls:*
  Action Plans for Touching Your Community
- *unLearning Church:*
  Just When You Thought You Had Leadership All Figured Out!

With more to follow!

Keeping Your Head Above Water: Refreshing Insights for Church Leadership
Copyright © 2002 Dave Stone

Visit our Web site: **www.grouppublishing.com**

Credits
Editor: Gary Wilde
Creative Development Editor: Paul Woods
Chief Creative Officer: Joani Schultz
Copy Editor: Candace McMahan
Art Director: Helen H. Harrison
Assistant Art Director: Jean Bruns
Cover Art Director: Jeff A. Storm
Cover Designer: Ray Tollison
Illustrator: Steve Bjorkman
Computer Graphic Artist: Tracy K. Donaldson
Production Manager: Peggy Naylor

Unless otherwise noted, Scripture taken from the HOLY BIBLE, NEW INTERNATIONAL VERSION®. Copyright © 1973, 1978, 1984 by International Bible Society. Used by permission of Zondervan Publishing House. All rights reserved.

Library of Congress Cataloging-in-Publication Data
Stone, Dave, 1961-
    Keeping your head above water : refreshing insights for church leadership / by Dave Stone.
        p. cm.
    Includes bibliographical references.
    ISBN 0-7644-2357-6 (alk. paper)
    1. Christian leadership. I. Title.
BV652.1 .S75 2001
253--dc21
                                                                2001054345
10 9 8 7 6 5 4 3 2 1   11 10 09 08 07 06 05 04 03 02
Printed in the United States of America.

Contents

Dedication

This book is dedicated to Wayne B. Smith, minister, Lexington, Kentucky.

Wayne, years ago your willingness to mentor a twenty-year-old Bible-college student was pivotal to my future service. Thanks for loving Christ, giving generously, and serving others. In fifty years of ministry, *you've kept your head above water* and inspired me to lead.

Getting Wet

I'm not the first person to use water to convey leadership lessons. Jesus loved the water. He fished, taught from a boat, calmed storms, and literally went for an evening stroll on the water! The seven stages of leadership you'll explore in this book were born out of my own experience with water-skiing. In each chapter we'll apply the original story (which I'll tell in Chapter 1) to your unique tasks in leading. Unfortunately, in church ministry we often find ourselves struggling just to keep our heads above water.

In a recent business book, fifty leaders of worldwide corporations were asked about the reasons for their success. When asked what one thing was the most important to them, the majority answered, "My own growth." At first blush, this response may seem self-centered. But the longer we lead, the more we tend to become set in our ways. Those fifty businesses couldn't grow if their leaders weren't growing too.

Of course, it is natural to play to your strengths and avoid your weaknesses. So don't become discouraged. Just realize that some of these chapters will affirm you in the work you're doing while other chapters will challenge you and motivate you to improve.

I believe the leaders who will have the biggest impact on the world of the future—a world that desperately needs Christ—are those who are *learners* more than *knowers*. They are willing to learn from one another. They are passionate about learning from their mistakes as well as their successes. And they constantly choose to put themselves in learning environments.

These are the trusting folks who can learn from their fears—just when they're afraid they're about to go under.

But they hang on to the rope and move forward anyway.

Is that you? Are you ready to launch into more effective leadership in the church, in spite of your fears? If so, then follow me...to the water!

CHAPTER ONE

The Whole Watery Story

Can I really do this, or will I blow it for everyone else?

It was our summer vacation, the first weekend in July, in beautiful Kentucky. The state is known for its scenic lakes, and one of the most picturesque is called Rough River. That may sound strange, but in Kentucky, a lake called a river doesn't seem all that odd.

Our gracious hosts were Dorris and his wife, Mary. When we arrived, they casually mentioned that their neighbors on the lake were members of a professional skiers club. Each year, on the Fourth of July weekend, the club members skied around the lake with as many potential new members as they could get on the water at once—all being pulled by one boat. *This I've got to see*, I thought. I secretly wished that somehow I could be included in this water-skiers' rite of passage.

But why would they choose me? After all, my skiing experience was limited to once or twice a summer. I wasn't a member of a professional skiing club, I didn't know these people, and they certainly didn't know me.

Nevertheless, I chose to hang around on a nearby dock when the group began to assemble...

Who's Available?

My adventurous spirit compelled me to at least see this strange, multiple-skier event. The best-case scenario would be to observe it on a pair of skis from behind the boat! While it seemed impossible that they would select a total stranger, it couldn't hurt just to be there. Good things might happen.

Mary called to her neighbor, "We have one who is willing to go if you need another."

My ears perked up, and my spirit lifted, until I heard the reply: "Thanks, but I think we're OK."

Members of my family were swimming nearby, and they encouraged me to join them. But, like an obstetrician on call, I said, "I think I'll just stay here in case they need me." The longer I sat there, the more foolish I felt. The skiers were hopping into the water. The boat was revving up. I looked like the new kid in town standing on the side of a sandlot ballgame, hoping against hope to be included.

Then Andy, the man who was organizing the event, yelled over to Mary, "We have an extra rope if you have someone!"

My heart beat faster. *Have someone?* Of course they had someone—me! You see, risk is my middle name. My shirt was off, my ski vest was on, and I was in the water before Andy could uncoil that rope. As I adjusted my skis, however, I did have a fleeting pang of doubt. *Can I really do this, or will I blow it for everyone else?*

I watched as a deeply tanned young lady tossed out 75-foot ski ropes to my nine bobbing partners. She looked like a cowboy swinging a lasso. With each throw, she landed a handle directly in front of a skier.

The others weren't nervous, but I was becoming concerned. You see, I didn't letter in four sports in high school. I'm athletic, but I'm no jock. Years ago I played college basketball, but these days my idea of exercise is filling the tub with hot water, pulling the plug, and fighting the current.

KEEPING YOUR HEAD ABOVE WATER

Anyway...I had jumped in the water to hide a recently grown belly that for some reason didn't fit very well under my ski vest. But I knew I could still ski! *After all*, I thought, *water-skiing for short distances merely requires a little basic coordination and a decent boat driver.* On those counts I felt OK.

So many thoughts swam through my mind. *They're all better skiers than I am. They've had a lot more experience and training.* A quick glance at my toothpick-shaped biceps reminded me that these guys were also in much better shape. How did I end up out here with the "big boys"?

The time had come, but my second thoughts continued bubbling to the surface. Darts of doubt and inferiority began to plague me. (I'd felt inferior before. In sixth grade I showed my dad my report card, which revealed four F's and one C. He said, "How do you explain this?" I answered, "I guess I spent too much time on that one class.") My deep-seated feelings of inadequacy began to escalate as liftoff drew near. I had no idea what I was doing or what was about to happen. But then someone yelled, "Everybody ready? Let's go!"

> ●
> The time had come, but my second thoughts continued bubbling to the surface.

The engine roared, and the boat began to pull us up—very slowly. Kevin, my new friend on my left, popped up for a second, thanks in part to his two wide skis—they resembled barn doors. But the speed was too slow, and Kevin quickly came back down. As he did, the guy on my right popped up. For a few seconds he enjoyed the thrill of being the first in the group to stand and ski. Then the boat's motor began billowing thick, black clouds of smoke.

All ten of us sank slowly into the water. The applause of our "fans" along the shoreline died out and gave way to questions and snide remarks. The driver told us not to worry; he thought he could fix the problem. The assorted families and onlookers, now about a hundred yards away, lost interest and returned to sunning, swimming, and chuckling at the ten ski-vested dreamers bobbing in the water. Our great plans had been rendered obsolete. We now had to lay back in the water and wait...and wait some more.

By now we had dishpan hands. The first strategy hadn't worked, so the people in the boat changed strategies—and props—and prepared to try again as the ten of us floundered and made small talk. Actually, I was intent on gaining helpful tips should our vessel regain power. I wanted my maiden journey to be successful. I innocently asked, "Is that boat really powerful enough to pull us up?"

"You know, it's a Malibu," said one of the guys on my right. "And it's got a 250!" His look of excitement let me know I should act impressed. "What did you think it had?" he inquired.

Wanting to prove I wasn't a complete doofus, I answered, "A 220, or 221—whatever it takes." (That line had worked in *Mr. Mom*, so it was worth a try.) He laughed, thinking I was making a joke. I'd dodged a bullet, although at the time I was totally unaware of the power I'd witness in short order.

Patience Pays Off

The twenty-minute delay was a blessing in disguise, since it gave me the opportunity to gather information and tips in the event we ever became vertical. My new buddies were quite helpful. They wanted to see me succeed, so they were happy to help. They knew all too well that if one skier went down, it could quickly become a game of Dominoes.

> ●
> They knew all too well that if one skier went down, it could quickly become a game of Dominoes.

"Remember, don't rush it," they told me. "Just let the boat pull you up."

Showing signs of nervousness, I asked, "How will I know when to stand?"

They glanced at one another confidently and, nearly in unison, replied, "You'll *know!*"

Soon the skipper yelled, "Everybody ready?" and shoved the throttle down. In a matter of about fifteen seconds, ever so gradually, *up from the waves we arose.*

I used my peripheral vision to make certain everyone had made it up. Like a parent in a delivery room checking for toes or fingers, I counted to ten. The people on the boat started cheering. Our families at the dock were ecstatic. We were euphoric. We were up! We were cruising! For a youth pastor it was the equivalent of a suc-cessful mission trip. For a preacher it

was Easter Sunday. For an elder it was that moment in the board meeting when the chairman finally says, "Since there's no further business, let's close with prayer."

In water-skiing, as in flying, the takeoff is the most danger-ous time. As we stood upon the water, in my mind's eye I saw images of Bill Murray playing the character Bob Wiley in the movie *What About Bob?* He was attached to a mast on a sailboat shouting, "I'm sailing! I'm sailing!"

Hey, I'm skiing! I'm skiing!

When it became evident that we were all actually going to stay up, Kevin, on my left, reached over and gave me a high five. Mine was not a confident high five. It was a mixture of fear and relief. We'd been patient and had finally managed to stand up together. Thus we had bonded and were now part of a fraterni-ty that few could claim as their own. Like ministers who have never exaggerated about an attendance count, we were the few, the proud, the skiers.

A Battle for Balance

The longer we skied, the more I realized the fight wasn't mere-ly against the water. I also had to battle the danger from the people on my right and left in this newly formed aquatic king-dom. After we had been traveling for a while, about seven of the skiers moved so close together that their skis were touching those of their neighbors.

In a purely egotistical attempt to be accepted, I tried this close-fellowship type of skiing myself. I am embarrassed to admit that the attempt was short-lived. In fact, when adjacent skiers came close to me, my body started to tense. I fought for balance as never before. Almost instinctively, I moved away in an effort to keep a relatively safe distance between us. When I saw that my territory was being invaded, I was immediately thrown out of my comfort zone.

It's tougher to keep your balance when you're stressed than when you're relaxed. Like a toddler taking herky-jerky steps, I began to feel pressure to keep my balance. I chanted the Weebles motto to myself: *Weebles wobble, but they don't fall down.* Was I a Weeble, or was I merely indulging in wishful thinking? It was too early to tell. Now for those of you who have never water-skied, let me get pretty deep with you: Keeping your balance is a very important part of skiing. (You can quote me on that if you'd like.)

The Pressure Builds...

I found my comfort level rising the longer I stayed above the water. But then to my left I saw a distraction. Boats that had passed us had turned around and were now racing alongside us. They came from the east, but they were not bearing gifts. These boaters were coming over to get a closer look at our strange, "out of water" experience. Some of the onlookers cheered; some waved; some took pictures.

But then we noticed that these gregarious sightseeing boaters weren't leaving. As a child, whenever I left for a sleepover at a friend's house, my parents would say, "Don't make them happy twice—happy to see you come and happy to see you go."

I could apply that piece of advice to the situation at hand. I wanted to see our onlookers go. While we enjoyed the momentary spotlight, these boaters were beginning to wear out their welcome. The more attention they paid us, the more pressure we felt. What had been commonplace—water-skiing—was now a performance, a challenging demonstration of skill under scrutiny.

And I noticed that the longer they stayed, the further we headed away from our resting place. At the time we didn't fully understand the price of our popularity, but the backtracking would add to our fatigue. Eventually the sightseers departed—making us happy twice, thus proving the truth of my parents' warning.

Teamwork Always Helps

Skiing straight across the lake was easy. I'd done it successfully in the past, so it was no big deal to stay above water. I felt comfortable with it. It was like riding a bike or juggling or slicing a tee shot; once a person learns how, it becomes second nature. So now that the other boaters had moved on, we were settling back into a straight, peaceful ride across quiet waters.

Or so we thought.

Our leader had other plans. The event was about to move from an individual sport to a team sport. What, you ask, could transform this collection of ten individuals into a team? The answer: making a turn and heading in the opposite direction.

Our ski-boat driver was excellent. He patiently waited for a spot with enough room to make the turn. He could have turned much sooner, but he would have lost two or three of us who were skiing on the outside edges of the column. We would have become living monuments on some dock or sandbar. Instead, he waited until the time was right and the setting could accommodate this radical, 180-degree change of direction.

Like it or not, we had to come together as a team at this point. If we all didn't do our parts, the Rough River church newsletter would record ten painful baptisms on that Saturday afternoon.

What makes the group turn so difficult is the mathematical reality that everyone is traveling at a different speed. The first skier on the far right is whipped across the wake at twenty-five miles per hour, while the skiers on the opposite side must fight to stay above the water at ten miles per hour. It quickly became apparent that turning takes teamwork. The only other alternative was to let go and watch our dreams sink. While my arms were aching, quitting didn't seem to be a viable option. It was sink or ski.

Of course, we really didn't have any say in the matter. Our leader, bone-dry and driving the boat, was calling all the shots. He didn't ask us where to turn—or even if we wanted to turn. He made the decision himself. Like loyal employees, we followed, thanks in part to the 75-foot ropes that were cemented into our rigor mortis–wracked fingers.

Just before going into the turn, our driver circled his forefinger two or three times above his head. This could mean one of two things. Either we were going to make a turn or he was singing "This Little Light of Mine" while doing the hand motions. Intuitively I sensed it was the former. He went into the turn, and we braced ourselves for a dramatic transition.

The turn was challenging and grueling. As we progressed through it, we encountered a new phenomenon: We were running smack-dab into waves we ourselves had generated! These were much larger and more powerful than the typical swells we'd been facing. Although we looked uncoordinated, somehow everyone managed to negotiate both the group turn and the massive waves from our own boat. Our path was now made straight, and we all breathed a secret sigh of relief.

We were still up; we were heading for home.

Faithfulness—Even in Fatigue

The longer I stayed above water, the better I felt. When I was able to block out my fatigue, the journey became enjoyable—even exhilarating. But there was no denying my exhaustion. My legs felt like jelly; my arms were like taut rubber bands. Yet I knew our achievement was about to be recognized and applauded. We'd entered the final quarter mile, the homestretch. Family and friends whom we'd deserted ten minutes ago were now coming into sight. Our accomplishment would become the small talk at summer parties and announced during conversation lulls at family reunions. If I could finish strong, the pain would be worth it. Seeing those folks in the distance gave me my second wind.

Surely I could remain faithful to the end. The fatigue and muscle aches became bearable as this light shone at the end of the tunnel. Our driver steered the boat past the dock where our families waited, and I quickly deduced his strategy. He was setting the stage for a dramatic, ten-person, up-close-and-personal drop-off.

now the drop-off in water-skiing is a tremendous ego boost for those who successfully execute it. But skiers can accomplish this maneuver only when they've perfectly executed the entire trip and *choose* to let go. Obviously, the drop-off isn't the result of losing balance; rather, it signifies that the accomplished skier has had enough and has decided that it's time to let someone else take a turn.

When the drop-off is correctly performed, the skier nonchalantly lets go of the tow rope and, for about three nanoseconds, resembles Jesus walking on the Sea of Galilee. Then, with an air of dignity and purpose, he gradually sinks. And he privately breathes a sigh of relief, knowing he looked so cool during the drop-off.

But please realize, there is no reason to drop off if you haven't mastered that look. It's the same look that comes over your face when the Sunday

●

But here's where the story heads south.

school superintendent attaches the 45-year-perfect-attendance pin onto your leisure suit. It's the calm, confident look of the high schooler who hits the game-winning free throw by banking it in. ("Yeah, I *meant* to do that.") Your goal is for observers to say, "Oh, he got bored, so he dropped off. Skiing for three miles doesn't even challenge him anymore."

I knew *the look*. It was filed in my memory bank, and I couldn't wait to pull it out and wear it proudly. The look would truly hide my internal disbelief that I had actually fought the good fight and finished the race.

But here's where the story heads south. It's Richard nixon before Watergate; it's Pete Rose before betting on baseball. The next paragraph will describe at least one reason you aren't reading this in "Drama in Real Life" in Reader's Digest.

You see, I never got to drop off.

I never got to display *the look*.

After I'd skied nearly three miles, the Lord summoned up a wave to humble me. This was to be my thorn in the flesh. As we approached the drop-off point, everyone was cheering, and some of us forgot the implications of turning. Remember the

KEEPING YOUR HEAD ABOVE WATER

part I described earlier when we hit our own waves? Well, the turn for the drop-off forced us to do it again. The first skier on the other side took a nose dive and, within seconds, the "wave for Dave" served its divine purpose.

Like the nonprofessional I was, I spun helplessly and hopelessly into the water. Submerged, I swallowed a gallon of refreshing Rough River. My head came out of the water just in time to see eight skiers cavalierly letting go, displaying *the look*, defying gravity for three nanoseconds, and honorably descending to the sound of applause and whistles.

Pushing skis before me, I dog-paddled the longest hundred yards of my life. I was thoroughly embarrassed and disgusted with myself. (Only those of you who are competitive can truly "feel my pain.") I oozed disappointment and anger. It was like making it through all the games and tournaments, only to lose in the state championship. My legacy would be all about "the one that got away."

In the homestretch I fell off the horse.

Go Ahead—Celebrate Anyway!

The others were out of the water and putting their skis away as I approached the dock. And there, to my pleasant surprise, supportive relatives and friends were heaping praise on me with only an occasional veiled reference to my humiliating splashdown. At first my pride got in the way, and I tried to slyly defend my drop-off, saying, "I saw the other guy go down and thought we all were supposed to fall so we wouldn't be too close to the dock." It was a gallant effort; the line had been thrown, but no one was biting.

You need to know that when we came into sight a quarter of a mile away, my sweet wife of fifteen years had begun video-taping our arrival. She had zoomed in for a tight shot of her beau as we approached the dock. The footage shows a wave coming at me. You can see a look of panic on my face, and you see me sail sideways and crash on my head. If you were to come to our house for dinner some night, she could show you that tape (if she ever discovers where I hid it). And you'd hear her off-camera disappointment: "Ohh, Dave just...*fell*."

Now as I stuttered before my dockside friends, it was obvious that the truth was known. My failure couldn't be lied away; it needed to be faced. Loved ones have seen plenty of my blunders, and one more wouldn't cause desertion. All they cared about was that I had done my best and made a memory that would last a lifetime. *I was so close! I can't believe I couldn't hold on for another five seconds!*

But the more I listened to my friends and family, the more I began to realize how much they wanted to focus on my victory even though I was fixating on my defeat. As I shared my disappointment with them, I wasn't wanting their pity; rather, I was searching for acceptance. It was a gift they graciously gave me. Comments such as "That's OK; I can't believe how long you all skied" helped to encourage me. They inspired me to dwell on the good memories, which I'm still enjoying.

> We laughed and smiled and relished our ten-minute lap around the lake.

During the rest of the afternoon and evening, we celebrated the experience. The story was told and retold. Questions were asked. I got to visit with some of the other skiers; they became friends instead of just numbers between one and ten. We laughed and smiled and relished our ten-minute lap around the lake.

❖ ❖ ❖ ❖ ❖ ❖

That vacation was months ago, and sometimes my family and friends still retell the story. Interestingly, they never mention the fall. They just tell about the three miles of water-skiing and omit the debacle of the final hundred yards. I can always tell whose version a person has heard when the story travels back to me. It's pretty easy to discern. The Dave Stone edition always includes the fall; the other versions graciously speak only of the journey. My "voyage to the bottom of the sea" for some reason didn't make their top-ten list.

I learned a lot that day. In fact, I'm still learning from my water-skiing adventure. Some of what I learned is about water-skiing; some is about leadership. Along with a mouthful of water, I absorbed seven distinct leadership lessons that day. (The preceding subheads may have already given you an idea of what those lessons involved.)

In the following chapters we'll be exploring seven key principles related to availability, patience, balance, pressure, teamwork, faithfulness, and celebration. Each principle will apply to you whether you're a pastor, a lay leader in your church, or even a Christian businessperson trying to run a secular organization in a God-honoring way.

So why not learn some leadership lessons on my dime? You won't need to take a crash landing in the lake to do it. You won't even need to get wet. All I ask is that, as you read this book, you keep in mind the kind of leadership skills that will make your own church or organization the very best it can be—and that you determine to grow stronger in those skills, day by day.

If you can do that, you will benefit. So will those who follow your lead. Then maybe all of us can keep our heads above water in this marvelous challenge of navigating the life of the church.

For Group Discussion

1. When was the last time you launched into a risky adventure? What happened?

2. When you think about being available for adventure, what is your overall attitude? How available are you at the moment?

3. In your church, what seem to be the greatest leadership needs? How have these needs become evident?

4. What do you hope you and your group will learn from studying this book together? What kinds of positive change do you envision as a result?

CHAPTER TWO

●

Available for Leadership

"We have one who's willing to go..."

My adventurous spirit compelled me to at least see this strange, multiple-skier event. Yet the longer I sat there, the more foolish I felt. The skiers were hopping into the water. The boat was revving up. I looked like the new kid in town standing on the side of a sandlot ballgame, hoping against hope to be included.

Then Andy, the man who was organizing the event, yelled over to Mary, "We have an extra rope if you have someone!"

My heart beat faster. Have someone? Of course they had someone—me!

❖ ❖ ❖ ❖ ❖ ❖

The longer I waited, the more I wished I had chosen to swim with my family. The whole thing was rapidly becoming an internal tug of war.

The "sure thing" versus the "risky venture."

When Andy said they could take another skier, my feelings became a mixture of excitement and twitching nervousness. Being a novice didn't do a whole lot for my confidence level! That description may fit your leadership ability; you may find yourself in unfamiliar waters. Leading a program at church or serving in a ministry can be frightening if you are inexperienced. Yet Christian organizations and churches will flounder and fail if there is no pool of available, capable "rookie" leaders.

Do You Have the Passion for It?

Sadly, it's becoming more and more difficult to find committed men and women to lead ministries—people who are willing to say no to the world's measurement of success and pursue God's plan for service. I'm talking about people with a passion to serve and lead, no matter what.

No, they're *not* the people who make pious statements about how much they've "given up" in order to be servants of God. Those individuals are masters at cleverly weaving their financial sacrifices into their testimonies. They constantly call attention to what they've forfeited so that God could use them. Lucky God!

When the righteous Ruler of the Universe sifts through our résumés, what is he looking for? I believe he seeks potential leaders who never specify where they will serve or how big their ministries must be. Oswald Chambers said, "God can do nothing with a man who thinks he is of use to God." Instead he is looking for people who can sincerely say, "I'll go where you want me to go, dear Lord, in spite of my weaknesses and shortcomings."

> The goal is for his plan to become your plan.

The term "available for service" loses all meaning if it's accompanied by a list of acceptable locations. In fact, God seems to enjoy putting people in settings they never dreamed of seeing. The farm boy ends up leading a metropolitan megachurch. The powerful attorney spends her weekends heading up the soup kitchen for the homeless. The class orator spends his years directing construction projects or writing. Before you present yourself as a candidate for kingdom service, remember that his ways are not your ways and his thoughts are higher than yours. Be open to God's leading, first and foremost. The goal is for his plan to become your plan. He's much less concerned with your *ability* than your *availability.*

If you're a baseball fan, you may recall an event in the fall of 1995 that attracted the attention of the entire sports world. Baltimore Oriole Cal Ripken played his record-breaking 2,131st consecutive game. His streak spanned thirteen years. During the media frenzy after the game, Ripken's mother told a story on television that I will always remember. It epitomizes the desire to be available. She said, "It was the night before Cal's first Little League baseball game. When I tucked him in that evening, I noticed he was wearing his baseball uniform. I told him he didn't need to do that; he'd have plenty of time to dress in the morning. So I made him get up and change into his pajamas."

Several hours later, before she turned in, Mrs. Ripken went in to check on Cal one more time. He was sound asleep, snug and comfy—in his uniform! He just couldn't wait for the morning to arrive. The boy wanted to be available for action. He had anticipated that game for so long that he wanted to be perfectly prepared at every moment.

Our world needs believers bursting with that kind of enthusiasm and availability. If it were the norm, the results would be far-reaching. Parachurch organizations would glow with vitality and vision. Churches would enter a new era of growth and excitement. Missionaries would be renewed in their callings and motivated to try creative new methods of outreach. Christian leaders would be making an eternal difference in the lives of others.

But you must sense that God wants to use you. I love the way Christian businessman Bob Shank puts it. He says, *"Career* is what you are paid for; *calling* is what you are made for." Do you have a passion to be a Christian leader and servant?

Don't jump into leadership until you have prayed and seriously thought it through. The person who says, "I would attend more and serve more if I had a leadership role," has it all backward. You can never rise higher in the kingdom than the level of faithful servant. You may teach a class, help lead worship on the music team, or be an elder or a deacon on the board, but if you are not willing to serve, then you won't be an effective leader. The Apostle Paul says, "Whatever you do, work at it with all your heart, as working for the Lord, not for men, since you know that you will receive an inheritance from the Lord as a reward. It is the Lord Christ you are serving" (Colossians 3:23-24). It's a great calling, but there are a few things ready to trip us up.

Beware These Devilish Barriers!

So many distractions can keep us from responding to Christ's call. I'm talking about certain menacing barriers to our legitimate desire to serve. If we're not alert and careful, they can hurl us into the waters of discouragement and drown a potentially thriving ministry. We could actually think of them in terms of doubt-inducing statements that Satan loves to whisper into our ears:

Barrier 1: **You don't have the talent!** When I was chosen to water-ski, my self-esteem began to fade. On the totem pole of talent, I ranked in the negative numbers compared to this group. The longer I waited, the more my mind generated sentiments such as *What do you have to offer? These guys and gals do this all the time. You're not qualified for Skiing 401. What are you thinking?*

Satan is an ever-present "help" in our time of need, isn't he? And naturally, his darts of doubt are often aimed at would-be leaders. He prompts us to ask ourselves, *Can I really do this...or will I blow it for everyone else?*

The devil is always ready to nurture feelings of inadequacy and convince us that our talents fall short of God's requirements. His favorite ploy in dissuading potential leaders is the comparison game. (He also uses this tactic against experienced leaders.) Several years ago, Christian author and preacher Max Lucado brought his elders with him to attend a leadership conference at Southeast Christian Church in Louisville, Kentucky, where I serve. While here, Max took part in a question-and-answer session that I moderated for several hundred ministers.

The pastors raised some great questions. I held the microphone as one gentleman asked what many were likely thinking: "Do you write your sermons first or your books first?"

Max responded, "Ninety percent of what I've written, I have already preached."

Everyone nodded in appreciation. I then took the microphone and said, "Max, I can say that too—because ninety percent of what you've written—I have already preached!"

Everyone broke into laughter because we could all relate. His material is so good that it continues to find a way into our messages. My point is this: I don't have the writing talent of a Max Lucado, but does that mean I shouldn't have written *this* book? (Don't answer that! I have feelings too.)

Satan loves to play the comparison game; God never plays. The Father wants you to rely on him, not on your talent. He wants you to *give* your talent, not compare it with other talents. He told Paul, "My grace is sufficient for you, for my power is made perfect in weakness." And Paul responded, "For when I am weak, then I am strong" (2 Corinthians 12:9-10).

> The Father wants you to rely on him, not on your talent.

Barrier 2: You don't have the discipline! *Will I be able to stick with this decision long after the initial excitement has faded?* That's a good question to ask ourselves. The "glory moments" in ministry are few and far between. In other words, I don't have to block out time to read all of the encouraging letters from people thanking me for my leadership.

At the core of self-discipline is the ability to make decisions rather than linger in procrastination. When he was a boy, former President Ronald Reagan went to a shoemaker for a pair of new shoes. The man asked young Reagan, "Do you want square toes or round toes?" Unable to decide, Reagan didn't answer, so the man gave him a few days to think it over. Several days later the shoemaker saw Reagan on the street and asked him again what kind of toes he wanted on his shoes. Reagan still couldn't decide, so the man replied, "Well, come by in a couple of days. Your shoes will be ready." When the future president did so, he found one square-toed and one round-toed shoe!

"This will teach you to never let people make decisions for you," the cobbler said to his indecisive customer.

"I learned right then and there," Reagan said later. "If you don't make your own decisions, someone else will."

Christian leadership requires effective decision making and a level of discipline that makes it possible. It also requires the discipline to "stick with it." In other words, leadership isn't something you can hop in and out of at your leisure. It serves no purpose to think you will lead for a few years then sit out for several years and then come back, be involved, and lead some more.

> Leadership isn't something you can hop in and out of at your leisure.

I heard about a woman who wrote a letter to the Internal Revenue Service saying, "Please remove me from your mailing list." Nice try, but it's not that easy! The same is true of leading in the Lord's work. When you make yourself available as a servant leader, you are saying, "I'm willing to take the steps to crucify my agenda and discipline my life to your will. Here am I, Lord—use me to your glory." As pastor and writer John Maxwell puts it, "Leadership isn't about titles, positions, or flowcharts. It's about one life influencing another."[1]

That doesn't happen on its own. It takes a firm commitment to God's goals and purposes. It takes discipline of mind, body, and emotions. But wherever you are when it comes to such lofty requirements, be not dismayed. You can immediately take the next step of growth toward greater discipline. Do it now, and ignore Satan's insidious whisperings. God himself will provide all you need as you step out in faith.

Barrier 3: **You don't have the knowledge!** I almost skipped the skiing opportunity altogether because I didn't know how to ski with a group. But if we allow ignorance to keep us from getting involved, we'll never try anything new, right? Potential lay leaders within a church fall into this trap when they say, "I never attended a Christian college" or "I've never taught a Sunday school class before." So what? Dive in and start learning.

Maybe you've heard about the unemployed man who learned of an opening for a janitorial job at a local church. The preacher asked him to fill out some employment forms, but the man said he couldn't read or write. The preacher then explained that the staff members wrote out their directions for the janitor, so he probably wouldn't be a good fit for the job.

However, wanting to be of some help, the preacher offered the man a basket of apples. The man ate a few and sold the rest to people on the street. With the money he made, he bought some more apples and sold those, too. With that money, he bought even more apples and eventually set up a profitable fruit stand on the corner. In a few months the fruit stand became a booming business and, after years had passed, the man was able to take a million dollars in cash to the local bank to open an account.

The banker asked him to fill out the appropriate forms.

"I can't read or write," said the man.

The surprised banker replied, "You can't read or write, and yet you've built a million-dollar business? Do you have any idea where you'd be if you were educated?"

"Yeah, I'd be the janitor at First Baptist Church!"

Knowledge isn't always the answer. God wants us to be willing to learn and to grow in knowledge, but he is glad to take us at whatever point in our lives we become available. Educational credentials certainly weren't imperative when God established the church. Luke writes, "When they saw the courage of Peter and John and realized that they were unschooled, ordinary men, they were astonished and they took note that these men had been with Jesus" (Acts 4:13). In this case, time spent with Christ carried more weight than a scholarly degree.

Jumping into leadership puts you on a path for growth. The teacher always learns more than the student because of the preparation required. When it comes to being a Christian leader, knowledge is nice, but it's not a prerequisite for signing up. Time will show that being a *learner* is much more important than being a *knower*. A learner continues to learn along the way, but a knower has arrogantly closed his or her mind to new ideas or methods.

Barrier 4: **you don't have the experience!** Perhaps you can recall a time you stood dockside as I did, contemplating a brand-new adventure. You were "chompin' at the bit" to be pulled into active duty for the divine. Maybe you were there, praying, hoping...and then *the call* came. Nothing else seemed to matter.

Yes, your mouth was desert-dry during that first sermon. Your knees knocked like castanets as you stood in front of the VBS class. Your voice wavered and cracked during the solo. But your chance had come, and you wanted to serve. Whether it was yesterday or decades ago, you probably remember every detail of your initial lurch into ministry.

When I was in school at Cincinnati Bible College, we ministry majors were required to complete a summer internship. One of the purposes was to expose students to the mountains and valleys of church leadership, giving us a thoroughly realistic view of ministry. How fortunate I was to be accepted to serve at the Southland Christian Church in Lexington, Kentucky.

Each night I recorded in my journal what I had learned about leadership, and I've benefited from those journal entries for years. At one point, I was on the faculty of a senior high camp week. This is what I recorded in my journal late one evening:

> **Little becomes much when you place it in the hands of God.**

"I spoke at campfire tonight. I didn't get to practice my message ahead of time. I had notes in my Bible and a flashlight, but I didn't end up using either. In the background where I stood there were three illuminated crosses. The Holy Spirit was in me, and I could feel him. I preached with more power than I ever have before. Five people came forward at the invitation. There is no doubt in my mind that I will preach the gospel until the day I die."

I was beginning to discover that a key ingredient in church leadership is something everyone can understand but not everyone is willing to do: *Simply be available.* I learned that night what Dwight L. Moody meant when he said, "God can strike a mighty blow with a crooked stick." On the lake I didn't need to be a professional skier, and in the church you don't need to be a seasoned veteran. You just need to make yourself available to serve God with a sincere heart.

You see, when you're inexperienced, it's easy to listen to Satan's whispers. But for the kingdom's sake, don't listen. The reason is simple: Little becomes much when you place it in the hands of God. A young boy with two fishes and five loaves of bread learned that lesson, and so must we. For every church member, the challenge is making the move from being a pew potato to a positive participant. For paid Christian leaders, the challenge is to move from seeing your work as a job to seeing it as a ministry, regardless of your level of experience.

But Are You Willing to Follow?

I've often wondered what would have happened if I hadn't been ready and waiting on the dock that day. What if I hadn't responded when I was called? What if I hadn't been there at all? Charles Swindoll writes, "Sensitivity has a Siamese twin—availability. There's not much good in hearing God's call if you're not willing to follow it when it comes."[2]

Another of my favorite authors, Philip Yancey, says it like this: "It is the very ordinariness of the disciples that gives me hope. Jesus does not seem to choose his followers on the basis of native talent or perfectibility or potential for greatness. When he lived on earth he surrounded himself with ordinary people who misunderstood him, failed to exercise much spiritual power, and sometimes behaved like churlish schoolchildren...I cannot avoid the impression that Jesus prefers working with unpromising recruits."[3]

Jesus told his disciples that they didn't choose him; rather, he chose them. Joseph Parker, preacher at the City Temple Church in London, was once asked, "Why did Jesus choose Judas as a disciple? He knew Judas would betray him!"

Parker replied, "I admit, that's a mystery. But there's a greater mystery—why did Jesus choose *me*?"

The Lord can use any of us to help lead and grow his church if our motives are pure. But if our motives are not pure, then and only then, our talent, discipline, and knowledge may become barriers to producing spiritual fruit.

On General Sherman's infamous march to the sea, he and his men wrought destruction everywhere they went. One day they came to a farmhouse where a woman sat on the front porch. Sherman said, "Ma'am, you need to remove your belongings; we are going to burn this house down." She stood up with her broom in hand and defiantly held it in front of her.

"Ma'am, you need to leave now," he said again.

"I'm not moving," she replied.

Sherman chuckled and said, "Madam, do you think you can defeat the entire Union forces with a broom?"

"No," she said. "But I want the world to know whose side I'm on." You may not be heralded as a "leader of the land." You probably won't receive the applause of thousands. But God is counting on you to make yourself available for his use. He's truly concerned with whose side you're on. So if you've been considering going into service for him, it's time to enlist. How great it would be if the angels could tell the Lord, *"We have one who's willing to go, if you need another."*

For Group Discussion

1. In practical terms, what does "being available" mean to you? Can you give an example related to church leadership?

2. Which of the barriers are most relevant to your own situation? Why? What remedies are you considering?

3. Are any of these barriers clearly evident in the life of your congregation? What could be done to overcome these barriers in the potential leaders you see around you?

4. What are some of the most encouraging examples of availability you've seen in your church? What would it take to encourage more folks to overcome the devil's whispers?

5. What is your next step in becoming more available for the Lord's use? What is the next step for your church?

CHAPTER THREE

●

Patient in Leadership

"Don't rush it. Just let the boat pull you up."

My new buddies were quite helpful. They wanted to see me succeed, so they were happy to help. They knew all too well that if one skier went down, it could quickly become a game of Dominoes.

Showing signs of nervousness, I asked, "How will I know when to stand?"

They glanced at one another confidently and, nearly in unison, replied, "You'll know!"

❖ ❖ ❖ ❖ ❖ ❖

It used to be that if people missed a stagecoach, they'd just wait a few days for the next one to come along. Now, in our fast-paced society, if we miss one panel on a revolving door we're frustrated. Richard Swenson, in his book *The Overload Syndrome*, writes:

"Even our sentences are peppered with such words as *time crunch, fast food, rush hour, frequent flyer, expressway, overnight delivery, and rapid transit*. The products and services we use further attest to our hurry: We send packages by Federal Express, use a long-distance company called Sprint, manage our personal finances on Quicken, schedule our appointments on a DayRunner, diet with SlimFast, and swim in trunks made by Speedo...

"We live in a nano-second culture, wheezing and worn-out...I have thought long and hard about the issue of speed and have come to believe that it is as much responsible for the problem of personal and societal dysfunction as any other single factor. Virtually all of our relationships are damaged by hurry."[1]

No wonder Jesus said, "Do not worry, saying, 'What shall we eat?' or 'What shall we drink?' or 'What shall we wear?' For the pagans run after all these things, and your heavenly Father knows that you need them" (Matthew 6:31-32).

Ever in a Hurry?

In today's society we "run after" many things. Is your engine ever running just a bit too fast? To find out, take this little quiz I've developed to measure your PQ (Patience Quotient).

1. Have you ever left a restaurant because a server took too long to take your order?

2. When reading a bedtime story to your child, have you ever tried to skip a page or two to expedite the process?

3. Have you ever hung up on someone while he or she was still saying goodbye?

4. Have you ever put your makeup on, or tied a necktie, while driving to work? (If you've done both, you may need to see a counselor.)

5. When you see a yellow light, is your normal tendency to accelerate instead of brake?

6. Have you ever wanted to reconfigure a long line at a wedding reception in order to go through more quickly?

7. Have you ever changed clothes while driving from the office to the golf course? (If I ever die in a car wreck—and I'm wearing my underwear and one golf shoe—you'll know why!)

8. Have you ever asked yourself during a sermon, *How much longer is he going to talk?*

9. Have you ever cut through a parking lot in order to miss a stoplight?

10. Do your children think their first names are "Comeon," "Hurryup," and "Letsmoveit"?

Count your yeses and grade your own paper. If you scored three or fewer, you have just tested out of this chapter, and you may proceed to the next. (But first make certain you have a pulse!) If you scored between four and six, you're probably normal in our fast-paced society. If you scored seven or eight, you're flirting with a dangerous habit, and you need to take steps to slow down. Finally, a score of nine or ten means you will need to read this chapter twice and contemplate making some major changes in your life.

When you're in a group water-skiing venture, patience is a tough pill to swallow. Waiting fifteen seconds to emerge from an underwater world doesn't sound like very long—unless you're one of the people swallowing all that lake water. But out on the lake that July afternoon, I wanted to avoid the most common faux pas in water-skiing: standing up too soon. (Four out of five dentists surveyed say that most rookie skiers fall and fail because of a lack of patience. Boat drivers can say it in their sleep: "Don't rush it. Let the boat pull you up.")

> ●
> **Microwaving leadership is like microwaving chicken—neither result is palatable.**

But it goes against our culture to wait. Max Lucado says, "America—the country of shortcuts and fast lanes. We're the only nation on earth with a mountain called 'Rushmore.'"[2] The idea of sharpening your ax isn't nearly as enticing as seizing the opportunity to hit the tree and make some chips fly. But there are few shortcuts. Microwaving leadership is like microwaving chicken—neither result is palatable.

Once you've thoroughly delved into your own crazy tendencies to hurry and rush, there are a few other things you need to know. We'll examine them in the rest of this chapter. If you want to become a good, patient leader, you'll need to become an expert at (1) knowing the unique purposes of priest-time and prophet-time, (2) knowing the difference between patience and passivity, (3) knowing what it means to wait for God's timing, and (4) knowing how much better it is to *receive* than to *rush*.

Time for a Priest or a Prophet?

Being patient in leadership requires the wisdom to understand what psychologist Jim Oraker calls "leading versus guiding." There are times when we need to be up front, leading people toward a goal. There are other times when we move alongside, guiding the team and orchestrating the members' combined giftedness. At first glance it may not appear that you are the leader in such a situation, but upon closer observation your leadership is obvious to those involved in the effort.

Back to our aquatic analogy. When you're in a crouched position seventy-five feet behind a boat, and the boat begins to drag you through the water, your success depends on the proper sequence of two impulses: the need to be patient and the desire to be bold. In other words, there's a time to sit and a time to stand. My preacher friend, Rick Atchley of Fort Worth, Texas, has a unique way of explaining this concept. He says that throughout the life of the leader there is an ongoing tension. It pulls us between being seen as the priest who lovingly ministers to the flock, and acting as the prophet who boldly challenges them.

This reality demands that a transition take place in virtually every ministry. Over the course of time in any growing organization, the leader typically moves from being a priest to being a prophet. The problem is that there are a lot of preachers who *start out trying to be a prophet* and telling people what to do. But it's often too early for that. These preachers haven't earned the right to be heard. Respect and credibility are the result of years of being a loving pastor and priest to the people. Only through years of faithful ministry does one earn the right to be heard as a prophet.

Other pastors have served faithfully for years in a priestly role, but now their congregations are looking for prophetic leadership, longing to be challenged. These preachers, however, are content to remain "crouched" in the security of their priestly positions rather than standing up to be the prophets God has called them to be.

Patient or Just Passive?

While patience is essential for a Christian leader, it is not to be confused with passivity. When the time is right to make a decision, you had better be willing to act. The Apostle Paul says, "Put on the full armor of God, so that when the day of evil comes, you may be able to stand your ground, and after you have done everything, to stand" (Ephesians 6:13). Every situation is different, but when it's time to stand—stand.

As in water-skiing, the challenge is knowing when to stand and trust that you can make your voice known and effective. A powerful boat can pop a skier up in two or three seconds, but to organize and pull off the "lifting" of an entire group of people, with their myriad visions and values, takes time. It won't happen overnight. It requires patience. Many pastors fall during the "takeoff" because they lack patience.

By the same token, some don't last in ministry because they try to stand too quickly. Their attitude is "Skip the prayer and the preparation. Who has time for patience?" Impatience spells disaster for water-skiers as well as leaders.

In 1998 I preached on several controversial topics in a sermon series titled "Moral Issues: Stepping Up and Speaking Out." Those messages would not have had as much impact on our church during the first year of my ministry in Louisville as they had after many intervening years. But through the years, the priest at times must step up and be the prophet. I like to describe my observations from twenty years of ministry with a simple equation:

Longevity + Integrity = Credibility

You see, Satan likes to tempt leaders to shy away from the tough issues. He whispers, "Don't rock the boat. Your job is to keep the peace." But passivity is not patience. An old country preacher used to say, "Silence isn't always golden; sometimes it's just plain yellow." If biblical teaching is being compromised, then it's time to stand up.

Years ago our church moved into a new building that was supposed to last us a lifetime. But after a few short years the handwriting on the wall became legible: It was time to build again. The only problem was that we had been in our new church building for only four years!

As in most cases, the staff (who were in and around the building each day) realized the inevitable before the lay leaders or the congregation. (Having your office in a closet has a way of driving home the need to expand. And in two of the worship services, some people had to sit on the steps instead of in pews.)

Bob Russell, our senior minister, encouraged the staff to continue to pray and wait. And Bob's plea for patience was just what we needed. The elders, deacons, and members all had to feel the cramped conditions for themselves. We had four services every Sunday, all the while realizing it was a Band-Aid remedy and not a long-term solution.

> As with my water-skiing group, the time had come to stand.

Then one day during an elders meeting, one of the men said, "What are we going to do about space? We have to do something dramatic, or we'll stop growing." The leadership promised to pray about the problem during the coming month. We investigated the options, too: Should we build a new sanctuary or add on to our existing facilities? The question began to gnaw at the leaders.

It was for that moment that the staff leadership had patiently waited. As with my water-skiing group, the time had come to stand.

We spoke up, saying to the elders, "We have some ideas." Our ideas weren't anything great, but when coupled with the expertise of lay leaders and the vision of a godly eldership, the plan began to materialize. A search committee was formed to find property in the direction the city was growing. After spending a year exploring, negotiating, being rejected, and walking forty parcels of land, we were led to just the right spot—eight miles away.

In the meantime we systematically paid off a twenty-year mortgage in just seven years. Extra monies were then aggressively applied to the purchase of land. We began a capital campaign to raise the necessary funds. Our goal of $26 million at that time, in 1994, was the largest amount any church had ever attempted to raise in a capital campaign.

In Ephesians 3:20 the Apostle Paul tells us that God "is able to do immeasurably more than all we ask or imagine." That is precisely what we experienced. Overnight an already generous congregation doubled its giving. Due to slower site work and longer construction than we had anticipated, a three-year capital campaign was prolonged to five years. It resulted in $40 million dollars being given to the building program—*over and above regular giving to the general budget.*

Your Flashlight or God's Floodlight?

Here's a question to ponder: What would have happened if we had tried to lead when we wanted to lead rather than when God wanted us to lead? Without the congregation's "buy in," the project would have flopped. Patience was required so that hearts could be prepared to sacrifice.

Of course, being patient enough to remain seated isn't easy. But if you are following God's timing, then patience pays off when it does come time to stand. God has a floodlight; we have a flashlight. One step at a time is the course for the patient leader who wants to walk and lead according to God's will. Time is relative to God. What seems a long time to us is a short time to the One who has been here for eternity. Trust his plan and his timing. He is never late and never early.

John Ortberg wrote a great chapter on rushing through life in his book *The Life You've Always Wanted.* He says, "We worship at the shrine of the Golden Arches, not because they sell 'good food,' or even 'cheap food,' but because it is 'fast food.' Even after fast food was introduced, people still had to park their cars, go inside, order, and take their food to a table, all of which took time. So we invented the Drive-Thru Lane to enable families to eat in vans, as nature intended."[3]

Two decades ago, time-management experts suggested that modern technology and shortcuts would reduce the average workweek from forty hours to approximately thirty-six hours. But just the opposite has occurred. The average workweek for salaried positions is over forty-six hours.

If you were to ask your co-workers if your behavior is generally patient or impatient, which attribute would be on the tips of their tongues? The majority of ministry occurs while you are in a holding pattern, simply waiting...waiting for a word of encouragement...waiting for a word of thanks for your willingness to volunteer as a lay leader...waiting for additional staff...waiting for the raise you were promised...waiting for the song to end so you can preach...waiting for the sermon to end so you can sing!

Simply put: It's all about waiting for God's time.

Rushing or Receiving?

Years ago I heard a youth minister named Paul Schlieker say, "If patience is the fruit of the Spirit, then hurry is not." Wow! The point is, we really can't engineer our lives to *get* what we want— even if it's spiritual fruit; we can only receive the gifts God chooses to give.

What a lesson for every leader! Jesus always chose his words carefully, and he said, "The pagans run after these things" (Matthew 6:32). Jesus knows it is typical for the world to run after things that *he wants to provide.* Jesus is saying, "There is no reason to rush and race for food, clothing, or shelter. If you seek me first, those things will fall into place as gracious gifts."

> I can't think of a place in the Bible where we are told to run with God.

It's interesting that we are told to stand firm and we're told to walk with God. But I can't think of a place in the Bible where we are told to run with God. We are told to flee from evil, but nowhere are we encouraged to run to God. Walking will be just fine. That is a tough lesson for those of us who are driven, Type A personalities.

In fact, there is no biblical record of Jesus hurrying. There is but one instance of a *representative* God-figure running. That occurs in the parable of the prodigal son when the father, representing God, runs to greet his son. So the only time we see the Lord in a hurry is when he is welcoming home one who has strayed.

While you wait to be pulled up to a new level of service, you may feel insignificant. You may feel about as useful as an ashtray on a motorcycle. While you're anxiously waiting to lead, remember that you will receive your chance. Be prepared when the opportunity arises, but remember the great Elvis' warning: "Only fools rush in."

You can learn much by watching a patient leader during meetings. He or she listens with eyes and ears, nodding encouragement, just as involved when listening as when speaking. That is a sign of Christian maturity.

The leader who weighs in on every issue and has to be the first to speak probably isn't leading very many. I like to watch Bob in our elders meetings. These meetings may last three hours, but he may speak a total of only five to ten minutes throughout each meeting. His philosophy is *If things are going the direction you want them to, don't open your mouth and waste some of your influence by speaking up.* Bob feels that unnecessary talk diminishes his clout when it's time for him to speak up about something that truly matters to him.

The Bottom Line: Patience Precedes Influence

Joseph, son of Jacob, was a good example of a man whose patience paved the way for a lifetime of godly influence. His time as a slave, as a servant, and as a prisoner prepared him for effective leadership. And Joseph wasn't the only biblical figure who saw patience pay off with eternal dividends. God prepared Moses for eighty years then allowed him to lead for forty. Jesus waited patiently for thirty years before ministering for three.

Cassie Bernall, a Christian high school student who was shot and killed in Littleton, Colorado, was prepared for seventeen years...to lead for one minute! But that one minute had an eternal impact upon thousands. A.W. Tozer said, "The wheels of God's justice grind slowly, but they grind exceedingly fine." God has everything figured out according to his timetable, not ours.

The prophet Isaiah taught a lesson that applies to all Christian leaders who begin to feel antsy about the magnitude or meaning of their ministries. He wrote, "They that *wait* upon the Lord shall renew their strength" (Isaiah 40:31, King James Version, emphasis mine).

When I graduated from high school, my home church held a reception for all of the seniors and their families. The parents were asked to write down their favorite stories about their graduates. This is what my mom wrote:

> **God has everything figured out according to his timetable, not ours.**

"When Dave was five years old, I received a letter from my mother that confirmed our fears. She had finally asked the specialist if my brother, who had cerebral palsy, would ever be able to walk. The doctor had said, 'No.' My brother had reached the age of thirteen, and we all felt that that would be the answer, but the sureness of the truth sank in with great pain. I started crying.

"About that time Dave came into the room and asked, 'What's wrong, Mommy?'

"Fearing he might think it something even worse, I decided to tell him. I said, 'Grandmother asked the doctor if Uncle Greg will ever walk, and we know now that he won't.'

"Dave said, 'Never?'

"I responded, 'Never.'

" 'Not even in heaven?'

" 'Oh, yes,' I said, smiling. 'He'll certainly walk in heaven!'

"He looked straight into my eyes, and with a voice of compassion and strength, he said, 'Then we'll wait.' "

They that wait upon the Lord. Someday my Uncle Greg will run and not grow weary. He will walk and not grow faint. In the meantime, he patiently leads from a wheelchair, waiting for that day when, literally, he will stand.

Waiting is never fun. But when the wait is over, the time will come for you to stand.

Through years of observing people, I've learned that while leaders don't enjoy waiting, it can be the best thing to do. As you serve and as you lead, periodically the Holy Spirit will give you a nudge. Your heart will pound. It will become obvious that someone needs to lead and that God is counting on you. Sitting on the sidelines will begin to be uncomfortable for you because of what God has placed on your heart. You ask, "How will I know when to stand?"

You'll know.

For Group Discussion

1. When have you been most impatient in your personal life? in your ministry?

2. When have you seen impatience do its worst work? When have you seen patience work wonders?

3. What would it take for you to become a more patient person?

4. In which area of church life is more patience required these days? from you? from your leadership team? from others?

5. If your group were to pray for more patience right now, what topics might arise? Make a list!

●

CHAPTER FOUR

Balanced in Leadership

I fought for my balance as never before...

The longer we skied, the more I realized the fight wasn't merely against the water. I also had to battle the danger from the people on my right and left in this newly formed aquatic kingdom.

When I saw that my territory was being invaded, I was immediately thrown out of my comfort zone. It's tougher to keep your balance when you're stressed than when you're relaxed.

❖ ❖ ❖ ❖ ❖ ❖

Whether you're on skis or trying to lead a ministry through rough waters, it can be difficult to maintain your equilibrium. Sometimes you're pulled between the extremes of various callings. If you work with a parachurch organization, you know the tension that flows from being pulled in many directions. It's tough to keep your sanity—let alone your balance.

Work and Rest: Keep the Space

Part of the balancing act for Christian leaders is learning how to deal with a job that's never finished. There's always one more thing to do. Yet when we buy into that mind-set, we allow Satan to win a pivotal battle; he wants us to believe that the Christian life is about *doing* instead of *being*. Then a "works mentality" leads to frustration, guilt, and inferiority. In contrast, Christ wants us to use our spiritual gifts out of gratitude, not guilt; out of devotion, not duty. Without such balance, we will have scores of Christian leaders skiing around the lake, holding on for dear life, so exhausted that they're vulnerable to any approaching wave.

Simply put, we must learn to balance work and rest. We must learn to balance other-nurture and self-nurture.

Have you ever noticed that Jesus was a master of this kind of balance? He would spend an entire day healing people. Then he would withdraw from the crowd. At the height of his popularity, when everyone was clamoring to get close to him, he took time off to pray by himself (see Mark 6:46). Today's casual observer might say, "What's up with that?" Pretend you are one of the candidates in the final three weeks of a close presidential race. Can you imagine taking a day off just to pray and be by yourself? Ludicrous, you say—a sure death toll for that candidate. But in whose economy of things? The leader who schedules time for spiritual refreshment and personal renewal will fare much better in the final analysis than his exhausted opponent. He won't have any difficulty holding onto the rope, regardless of the choppy waters.

It can be difficult to determine whether our lives are in balance. Our society is notorious for moving from one extreme to another. In C.S. Lewis' book *The Screwtape Letters*, a senior demon by the name of Screwtape offers his nephew advice on how to tempt a human being. Screwtape says, "All extremes except extreme devotion to the Enemy are to be encouraged. Not always, of course, but at this period. Some ages are lukewarm and complacent, and then it is our business to soothe them yet faster asleep. Other ages, of which the present is one, are unbalanced and prone to faction, and it is our business to inflame them."[1]

Solomon advised just the opposite. Ecclesiastes 7:18 says, "It is good to grasp the one and not let go of the other. The man who fears God will avoid all extremes."

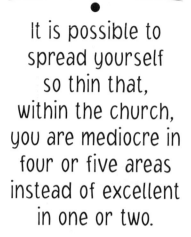

It is possible to spread yourself so thin that, within the church, you are mediocre in four or five areas instead of excellent in one or two.

Learn to balance your responsibilities. It is possible to spread yourself so thin that, within the church, you are mediocre in four or five areas instead of excellent in one or two. I've heard Rick Warren say, "People who burn the candle at both ends may not be as bright as they think they are."

Inevitably, there will be crunch times when your personal space and schedule are smothered. Although I feared falling when the other skiers got "up-close and personal" with me, I also enjoyed an adrenaline rush from this new sensation. If you love what you're doing, you can handle those busy times. Like the skiers who moved in on me, your leadership responsibilities will encroach upon your personal space. Then your main focus in ministry may sometimes get cheated. Your family may have to accept that the funeral is more important than the picnic—on that particular day. You may feel crowded and cramped, but if that is necessary to accomplish the larger goal, you endure it because you have the big picture in mind. But make certain this is the exception and not the norm. And make it up to your family.

When less hectic times finally arrive, it's no time to coast. Now is the time to catch up, dream, pray, and plan. Schedule time for the unexpected—and time to do some creative planning. An assistant can check back with you to see how you are progressing with a particular project and, given permission, can gently assist you in many other ways. A side benefit is that your assistant will feel valued as a partner in ministry rather than a subordinate.

Priorities: Don't Major in Minors

Because so many worthwhile needs call for our attention, we must prioritize. It's easy to major in minors, even in Christian work. If we're not careful, our efforts can appear just as foolish to the world as the anger of the religious leaders in Jesus' day over a healing on the Sabbath. They were majoring in minors. Oblivious to the obvious, they missed the miracle because they focused on the wrong thing.

As you serve the Savior, how would God have you spend your time? What are the greatest expectations and needs? What unique gifts do you have to offer?

The challenge for leaders of small organizations and churches is to prioritize and enlist volunteers to undertake secondary responsibilities. If you wear too many hats, you won't be able to effectively lead the church and maintain your sanity. The challenge for churches and large organizations is to maintain the level of excellence that people have come to expect. That means continuing to adapt and change methods while still concentrating on your strengths. This is where some of us church leaders begin to blow it. Busyness becomes a badge we proudly wear. We boast that we're busier than an octopus at a square dance, proudly proclaiming, "I'd rather burn out than rust out." But if we follow Jesus' example, we don't need to burn out or rust out!

There is a better alternative. Christ withdrew from the crowds because he knew he needed spiritual recharging. He prayed. He meditated. And he was able to complete his work. Satan would love to take your focus off the primary and place it on the peripheral. If he can't make you bad, he'll make you busy. But there must be a light at the end of the tunnel, or you will snap. An American Indian proverb says, "The bow will eventually break if you keep it always bent."

Growth can easily be stifled in church settings when lead ministers become inundated in minutiae. If duties aren't removed from their plates, they'll no longer be able to concentrate on their main purpose of preaching and casting the vision. As churches grow, this must be an ongoing task for the elders and deacons. By continually adjusting the balance, they ensure against their pastors' burning out or rusting out. Olan Hendrix wrote, "The very essence of staying focused is the avoidance of distractions. The culprit is not the obvious, but the subtle. The diversions we most easily rationalize are the most dangerous."[2]

Today's Christian leaders must have a plan for where they are going and focus on it. They need to ask themselves, *What can I do that others can't? Where do I need to concentrate my time and energy?*

Some churches stagnate because the lay leadership isn't willing to lighten the senior pastor's load. If a pastor's gift is preaching, then local leaders should try to assume other tasks so the pastor's

Recovering From Workaholism

Balance in ministry isn't necessarily an oxymoron. Here are six tips to ensure the ministry doesn't become more important than the Master.

1. Evaluate how you spend your time.

Once every year or two, conduct a personal inventory to determine how you spend your time. For two weeks, record, in thirty-minute increments, your activities. Use categories such as work, sleep, spiritual development, exercise, recreation, driving, family time, and eating. Seeing how your time is spent may reveal that your job is eroding important areas in your life.

2. Communicate how important your family is.

Let members of your family and staff know through your words and actions that your family comes before

your work. This message must be genuine, or it will be dismissed. One way that author and speaker Dennis Rainey communicates this message is by taking phone calls from his wife and children whenever they call, no matter with whom he is meeting. His instant accessibility assures his loved ones of their importance.

3. Eliminate what you can.

If I bring work home, I feel guilty if I don't work on it. If I do work on it, I feel guilty for not spending time with my family. Everyone wins when the work stays at work. Prayerfully prioritize your work, and do the most important things. The rest will wait.

4. Meditate through prayer and Bible study.

Many in ministry are running on empty. There is a great deal of truth to the old saying "It is impossible to lead someone to a place you have

KEEPING YOUR HEAD ABOVE WATER

preparation and study can be dedicated to honing that craft.

The longer you're up on skis, the more your hands begin to tire from gripping the rope. So you hold twice as tightly with one hand while giving the other a break. You know that if you can balance it out you'll be able to go further. If not, you'll burn out. Do the same in your labors for the Lord.

When it comes to priorities, please remember this: You can do *something*, but you can't do *everything*. Christian leaders need not fall into the trap that has swallowed up secular leaders in

never been." As a Christian leader, you must protect your time in the Word and with the Lord. The disciples asked Jesus to teach them how to pray (Luke 11:1). The psalmist said, "Blessed is the man... [whose] delight is in the law of the Lord and on his law he meditates day and night" (Psalm 1:1,2). Make your prayer and Bible study time a priority.

5. Recreate on a regular basis.

The constant pressures and stress of Christian leadership can wear you down. We all need some form of physical and mental recreation, which allows us to get our minds off of ministry. My escape is playing golf. When I play golf with Bob Russell, my ministry partner, I never discuss church problems—unless he's ahead in the final holes! Your body houses the Holy Spirit. The challenge is to be a good steward of all that God has entrusted to you. Whether you jog, lift weights, play tennis, or golf, just be sure not to let the diversion become an obsession.

6. Vegetate one day a week.

The Lord worked for six days and rested on the seventh. Why? Was God exhausted? Were God's muscles sore? Did the Lord just need a day to sleep late? Of course not. I think God did it to set an example for us. So take a day off and don't feel bad about it. If the Creator of the universe rested, then there's no reason to put yourself on a guilt trip for doing the same.

It is recorded several times in the Gospels that Jesus pulled himself away from the masses and the disciples for private times of spiritual and physical renewal. Mark 6:31 says, "Then, because so many people were coming and going that they did not even have a chance to eat, [Jesus] said to [the disciples], 'Come with me by yourselves to a quiet place and get some rest.' " Two thousand years ago, Christ's antidote for burned-out disciples was a little R & R. Perhaps that's what you need too!

search of worldly success. Your worth and significance need not be attached to your title, the size of your paycheck, or the number of hours you work. Rather, value is always determined by ownership. A jersey that belonged to Michael Jordan will be worth much more than one that you or I own. If you are a Christian, then you belong to Christ. You are highly valued, but not because of the tasks you perform or the size of your ministry. You are significant because you were bought by God at the cost of his Son's life. You belong to him.

Sometimes Christian leaders become so involved in the work of the Lord that they forget the Lord of the work. To-do lists and important responsibilities crowd out Christ. Quiet time becomes rushed or nonexistent. Bible readings become merely an opportunity to look for lessons to teach rather than to make personal applications. Chuck Swindoll reminds us that "noise and words and frenzied, hectic schedules dull our senses, closing our ears to His still, small voice and making us numb to His touch."[3]

Jesus talked to his disciples about maintaining balance. He said, "I am the vine; you are the branches. If a man remains in me and I in him, he will bear much fruit; apart from me you can do nothing" (John 15:5). In your quest to do the *good*, don't neglect the *best*. A river cannot rise any higher than its source.

"Are you living by the clock or by the compass?" asks Stephen Covey. "The clock represents our commitments, appointments, schedules, goals, activities—...how we *manage* our time. The compass represents vision, values, principles, mission, conscience, direction."[4] Often there's a gap between the two. The challenge is to live by the compass and not the clock. If you lead and serve with the compass in mind, it will be easier to prioritize and keep the big picture in plain view. The Christian should be the best volunteer or employee. He or she should work hard and be an extra-mile example to others. But the Christian must also learn to say no. If balance is missing, then the ministry will falter. More times than not, the home will get the short end of the stick.

Family: Shrink That Space!

Greg Leith directs leadership development for the Christian Management Association. He and his assistant created an ingenious and effective plan to limit the time Greg is away from his family each year. At the beginning of each year, they determine a maximum number of days for out-of-town travel. After placing that same number of marbles in a small crystal jar, Greg removes one marble each night he is away. When he is invited to give a speech, attend a conference, or visit a client, a quick glance at the jar makes his decision easy. What wisdom! Greg's goal at home is the same as every leader's: No one wants to hear a family member say, "Dad's lost all his marbles!"

It's often easy for me to forget that family comes before others in my labors for the Lord. It is a paradoxical mathematical equation: My first priority, upon which God will judge me, is a family of five rather than a congregation of fifteen thousand.

I heard of one minister's wife who threatened to put these words on her husband's tombstone: "Gone to another meeting." In sixteen years of marriage, my wife has heard me use that phrase with regularity to try to excuse a busy stretch, a misplaced priority, or a simple unwillingness to say no. I'm doing better, but my boundaries aren't where they should be. Creating appropriate "family margins" allows a marriage to flourish. Boundaries allow a Bible-school teacher to prepare more and observe more. It's much easier to be crowded if the crowding is on only one side and not on all sides.

I was fortunate to grow up in a preacher's home where my father was the same man in the pulpit that he was in the home. *Balanced* describes him well. One of my fondest memories from my youth is of the

> My father was the same man in the pulpit that he was in the home.

day my dad received a telephone call from the preacher of a large, well-known church. As I listened from the other room, I knew Dad was being invited to speak at that church. I thought,

This is great. Dad would love to speak there. Then I heard my dad repeat the date: "February third? I'd love to. Let me check; I'll be right back." As he went bounding up the stairs to get his calendar, my heart sank. I knew that I would be in a school program that very night. In a flash he came back down the stairs, flipping through the pages. He returned to the phone I listened from around the corner.

Dad said, "February third. No, I'm sorry, but I already have a commitment that day. Maybe another time." After some small talk, he closed the conversation and hung up the phone. Without even knowing it, he had communicated to me, "Son, I love you. You are more important than the opportunity to speak at a big church."

One of the reasons I wanted to follow in my father's footsteps in Christian leadership is that he put his family before the ministry. But that has not always been the case for me. For the first few years, I regularly worked sixty to seventy hours a week without a day off. And the fact is, down deep inside, I was proud of it. But the more I studied the Scriptures and was challenged by my accountability partner, I realized *shame* was a more appropriate emotion in my situation than *pride*. I was out of balance. While I am improving, I have a long way to go.

Early in my ministry I tended to ignore what my dad had modeled for me and fell into the unhealthy pattern of a workaholic. Climbing the ladder and being successful in ministry became my prime pursuit. While I still fight those inclinations, I'm seeing some improvement. I realize what I need to do. In the left-hand corner of my car's windshield is a sticky little square reminding me when to change the oil and balance and rotate the tires. That kind of maintenance is wise for me as well as for my car. On a regular basis I need to be recharged, rotated, and rebalanced—about every five thousand miles!

Recently I spoke at a Promise Keepers conference about men's need to balance our commitment to work with our commitment to our wives. This is what I said:

"The first two years of our marriage I worked for a Bible college. I considered 'time on the job' as a higher priority than time with my wife. Our marriage at that time wasn't as strong as it could have been, all because of me. We lived in northern Kentucky, and my wife missed her family desperately. She didn't know very many people, and I would come home for dinner to find her excited that I was home. But, on many occasions, I could tell she'd been crying. It would upset me to see her this way, but it didn't upset me enough to make me stay home—because I was *needed* back at work.

"Basically, I blew it.

"I finally realized something needed to be done. I went to the president of the college and said, 'I need to travel less and work less, because it's not productive for the spiritual climate of my marriage.' I knew that if you didn't nip this in the bud early, ten years later there's no marriage left.

"Thankfully, I was married to a woman who was and is a promise keeper. She didn't bail out on me early in our marriage. She's not in this building tonight, but do you know what she's doing while I'm speaking? She saw this as a teaching time for the family. She's not in here; she's standing out there—somewhere in the parking lot. And she is holding hands with an eleven-year-old, an eight-year-old, and a five-year-old. They are praying for their daddy, and they are praying for you."

Immediately after I uttered those words, all nineteen thousand men in attendance rose to their feet and gave my wife a standing ovation. It was a very emotional night for me. Afterward, I had difficulty trying to convince my wife that

> • **Praying is more important than preaching.**

she had had a greater impact on those men as she was praying in the parking lot than I had, standing in the pulpit. Yes, the men in that audience related to my confession about living a life out of balance, but they were more impressed with my wife's faithfulness and forgiveness.

Amid the rat race of your regular responsibilities, remember that praying is more important than preaching. That is how you can regain your balance.

Satan wants you to overdose on church at the expense of your loved ones. At times many of us have committed spiritual (or ministerial) adultery. We've lived as if we were married to the church. But the church is already married. The Bible teaches that the church is the bride of Christ. Perhaps you have a spouse and children who long to have the kind of access to you that your church members and constituents have. They long to feel they are *at least as important as the flock*. We may define success as working long hours and sleeping short nights. But if we climb to the top of the ladder and our loved ones aren't there beside us, then what have we really accomplished?

Maybe you have made some mistakes along these lines. As you've been reading this chapter you may have been thinking, *If I can just learn this lesson, then I don't need to read another page. Everything else pales in comparison to admitting I'm out of balance and need to change.* If that describes you and you are serious about being a godly leader, then start the change process right now. The Apostle Paul said, "Forgetting what is behind and straining toward what is ahead, I press on" (Philippians 3:13-14). We must *learn* from the past, not *live* in the past. Block out family time, and stick to your plan.

I've never heard a dying person say, "I wish I had spent more time at the office." The opposite is usually whispered.

Right now, ask God to change you through the power of the Holy Spirit. Confess your blunders to those you've squeezed out of your schedule. Strive to no longer hurt the ones you love the most. Fight for balance as you have never fought before. On the windshield of your mind, affix a reminder to stay in balance.

Ten Practical Tips for Balancing Ministry and Family Time

1. Date your spouse.

Even after you are married, you need to date your spouse. Schedule a night once or twice a month for a night out together, without the children. You and your children will benefit from making your marriage a priority. If you can't afford a baby sitter, find another couple with whom you can trade off baby-sitting duties.

2. Wherever you are, be *all* there.

When you are about the Lord's work, remember it is Christ you are serving. A poor work ethic invites ridicule and diminishes credibility. On the other hand, don't dwell on ministry problems and responsibilities after you leave the office. Flip off the switch when you head for home. If you're preoccupied, your time with your family won't really count. Let your loved ones know that they are truly cherished.

3. Eat dinner together.

A common thread among successful people is that most grew up eating dinner with their families. The benefits of eating meals with your family are both obvious and numerous: Manners are taught, principles are modeled, and lessons are learned.

4. Learn to say no *for* your children.

Many children want to be involved in everything. (Where do they learn that, I wonder?) Parents need to remember that, contrary to popular opinion, the world doesn't revolve around their kids' extracurricular pursuits. Help children prioritize their time with an emphasis on serving God with the gifts he's given them.

5. Never publicly ridicule your spouse.

Some Christian leaders regularly make fun of their spouses. Repeated personal illustrations—however humorous—can wound the ones you love most. Your congregation needs to know that you treasure your mate and would never toy with temptation.

6. Schedule dates with your children.

An out-of-town hospital call or a speaking engagement can provide a wonderful opportunity for you to spend quality time with one of your children. Buy a disposable camera so your child can chronicle the trip. I've found that my children will open up freely when it is "just us" for an extended period. For best results make sure the ratio is one parent to one child. *(continued)*

7. Take your children to a place that is special to them.

As I write this book, my three children range in age from six to twelve. About once every six weeks, I take each child to a special eating place that he or she has chosen. This location becomes a *sacred secret* that my kids do not disclose to one another. Each child gets to choose a different place twice a year. I'm noticing that the older they get, the more cultured their palates have become! McDonald's has given way to more expensive choices. My nine-year-old, Sadie, used to choose Applebee's. She loved the barbecued ribs. Once when Sadie and I returned from lunch, Samuel, my six-year-old, loudly declared, "Sadie, you ate at Applebee's." Like Simon Peter, she denied it three times.

Unconvinced, Samuel whispered to me, "Dad, her breath *smells* like Applebee's!"

8. Pray together each night.

If you are married, there is no better way to close out the day than to pray with your spouse. This involves your spouse in your ministry and allows you to pray for each other's needs. These prayers promote intimacy and foster commitment to God and to your marriage.

9. Turn the television and computer off, and play together.

Television stalls conversation and interaction. Use it sparingly. Couples and families who watch TV for extended periods of time or spend countless hours on the computer talk to one another less and less. Replace those hours with interactive activities that stretch your mind and creativity. You'll make memories that last a lifetime.

10. Keep the communication lines open.

The need to communicate doesn't end when you turn forty or when the kids grow up. Someone said, "If Adam had been talking to Eve, she wouldn't have been out in the garden talking to a snake." Guys, we need to be listening *and* talking. Communication is key to making a ministry marriage work.

When I was growing up, I was always intrigued by the personal attention my parents gave to each other. As we ate dinner together, my dad would pull an index card out of his pocket. On it would be a few words he had jotted down that day. Referring to the card, Dad would share events of the day or things he'd heard. He might say, "Jed Winston got season tickets to the Reds' games," or "A new Disney movie is coming out." Even now, Dad makes his list and goes over it with Mom. She knows that when he jotted something down, he was thinking of her. She knows that she was on his mind throughout the day, and that makes their moments together even more precious.

For Group Discussion

1. What principle or concept in this chapter had the greatest impact on you?

2. How would you describe your current balance between work and renewal? between majors and minors? between church and family? Can you share a specific example?

3. How well does your church's leadership team help protect the senior pastor's focus, time, and energy? What steps could be taken for improvement in this area?

4. As a result of reading this chapter, what one thing have you been inspired to do regarding your family life?

5. What could be done about the overall health of your congregation's family lives? Brainstorm some ideas!

CHAPTER FIVE

Pressures of Leadership

The more attention...the more pressure.
To my left I saw a distraction. Boats that had passed us had turned around and were now racing alongside us. Some of the onlookers cheered; some waved; some took pictures.

While we enjoyed the momentary spotlight, these boaters were beginning to wear out their welcome. What had become commonplace—water-skiing—was now a performance, a challenging demonstration of skill under scrutiny.

❖ ❖ ❖ ❖ ❖ ❖

Good skiers enjoy any attention that comes their way. There is a swelling of the head when people want to get up-close and personal to see the fabulous trick you're doing. The sight of one or two people skiing behind a boat doesn't turn a lot of heads. But the sight of ten people skiing behind one boat does capture significant attention. So that day on the lake, boats began following us. They took turns coming alongside so that their occupants could snap pictures.

KEEPING YOUR HEAD ABOVE WATER

In those Kodak moments when attention comes knocking, pressure often escalates. In fact, *leadership is always accompanied by pressure.* The person who has no supervisory responsibilities, no staff members reporting to him or her, often goes home at five and may not think about work until the next morning. This person may experience little, if any, work-related pressure. But it's different for leaders. The following five sources of pressure will pay you a visit on a regular basis if you are truly leading.

Pressure From the Spotlight

What would you have done had your boat passed us on that Fourth of July weekend? Would you have kept going? Would you have turned around to get a closer look? If you had the slightest interest in skiing, the sight itself would surely have piqued your curiosity. An attraction occurs when something ordinary is done in an extraordinary way.

I'll bet you've garnered a few stares along the way in your leadership efforts. Maybe the county newspaper wrote about your live nativity scene and quoted you. Perhaps a church from another denomination wanted to pick your brain on how to set up a fund-raiser. Or perhaps the local television station asked for your opinion on the relevance of the Bible in today's society. Whatever the angle or the audience, you and I have experienced times when people "pulled their boats alongside" to get a closer look at what we were doing. How you handle the pressure of the spotlight will help to define your future as a leader. Peter Drucker says, "Failures are self-correcting; it is success that will do you in."

Jesus knew what it's like to be followed. Crowds followed him wherever he went. His path was blocked when he was in the spotlight.

Those who serve in ministry already live in a fishbowl and find that extra scrutiny just adds more pressure to their job description. The spotlight allows people to gaze at the life of the leader, who may be unaware of how closely others are watching. *Your* heart may be right. *Their* motives may be sincere. But the result is still the same: added pressure.

For the past eleven years, I have served as the media spokesperson for our church. In the year ahead, that responsibility will become someone else's so that I won't be a lightning rod for controversial issues. As with the photo shoot initiated by the other boaters, these things usually start out as fun—until somebody "loses an eye."

Attention from the media quickly loses its luster. You have to view the interview as an opportunity to promote Christ or to do damage control.

The topics you're asked to address may seem far removed from your own situation, and you may be surprised what will bring the spotlight to your door. Be prepared; when you least expect it, expect it. Regardless of the size of your ministry, people will come with their baggage, and there will be all sorts of problems packed inside.

> •
> **Regardless of the size of your ministry, people will come with their baggage.**

The spotlight accentuates those problems. The spotlight certainly presented some problems for us skiers on the lake. We wanted to return to our families, but because there were ten of us, we could turn around only in the widest areas of the lake. If there was a boat alongside us, we couldn't turn at all. We had to keep skiing until we came to another wide spot and hope that the shutterbugs had gone on their way.

Being in the spotlight made us feel important, but it cost us time, added to our fatigue, and perhaps contributed to my fall. The same things happen in thriving ministries these days. Growth occurs and is followed by interest and notoriety, which increase the pressure, stress, and expectations, which can sometimes lead to a fall. There's an unsavory trade-off—the more success, the more scrutiny.

Preaching to five hundred is different from preaching to a hundred. The message and preparation are the same, but the pressure is different. The stakes are higher. Yet numbers aren't the only basis for how much we sweat. I might feel comfortable speaking to six thousand people in a worship service but get "dry mouth" when presenting an idea to fourteen elders.

Some scrutiny will come from the Christian community itself. That can be good pressure or bad pressure, depending upon the community's desire for unity. Nevertheless, it is still pressure. And the more successful and unique your team is, the more you will have to say no to outside opportunities to ensure continued success.

It's tough to keep your focus when everyone wants to get up-close and personal with what you are doing. That's why many churches (Willow Creek, Saddleback, Southeast, Ginghamsburg) have started their own leadership conferences. Otherwise they'd be filling up their weekends answering the questions of curiosity seekers instead of pouring their energies into those who come to be spiritually fed. These biannual conferences prevent these churches from being encumbered by the "boats alongside." If churches neglect their ministries and spend all their time sharing their stories, pretty soon they won't have stories to share.

At times, the spotlight that creates the most pressure doesn't come from the media or from other churches; it emanates from our own constituencies. It's the treasurer who questions you on every receipt you submit for reimbursement. It's the chairman who micromanages instead of giving you appropriate freedom. It's the board that wants to know how many calls and hospital visits you made last week.

But the worst source of pressure can be hiding in your shirt pocket.

Pressure From Your Day Planner

As you know, those of us in ministry are bombarded with responsibilities and invitations. It's nice to be included, but the pace can drain us if we're not careful.

Just say no.

Recently I was asked to speak to one of our church's twenty

support groups. About a year ago, I'd decided that I had better say no to this kind of request. While I enjoy the opportunity, it isn't fair to my family. And once I've spoken to one group, it's unfair to refuse the next. The man who asked me was hopeful, but after I took the time to share my predicament with him, he said, "OK, I understand. I appreciate your taking the time to explain it to me. It makes sense to me now."

Not everyone will be so understanding. Some will grumble behind your back. But you have to establish your priorities, or you won't last in the ministry. If you are too nice to say no, then *just don't say yes*. Ask these people to call your assistant, and teach that individual to say no for you! As I mentioned earlier, you must continually prioritize and remove tasks from your plate.

Elders and deacons, you must take the lead in reducing your pastor's duties.

> ● **If you don't plan your schedule, others will!**

Most pastors will counsel some of their church members. I have chosen not to do marriage counseling, and I have the blessing of my elders in this decision. Others handle that ministry full time. Since counseling is neither my strength nor the priority of my ministry, diverting an hour or two from my sermon preparation for counseling is the equivalent of investing in a couple at the expense of the fifteen thousand who will hear the sermon that weekend. In rare circumstances I have made such a trade-off. But if you are the preacher, and that kind of "stolen time" becomes the norm, the quality of your sermons will diminish. No one will say, "Pastor Bill wasn't as sharp today, but I understand that he really helped the Wilsons with their marriage."

It doesn't work that way.

Does that sound cold? The Apostle Paul encouraged the church at Ephesus to "[make] the most of every opportunity" (Ephesians 5:16). As a leader you have no other choice if you desire to maximize your effectiveness.

Let me put it another way: *If you don't plan your schedule, others will!* The size of your ministry has absolutely no bearing on this principle. Ask yourself what you can delegate to volunteers or staff members so that you can turn your attention to what you do better than anyone else in the organization. For example, your gifts, passion, and schedule may lead you to counsel couples. That's great, but find things to remove from your schedule so you can concentrate on the things you have deemed most important. When you stand in the pulpit, you will realize how wise you were to block out study and prayer time earlier that week. That time is what enables you to deliver what the Holy Spirit has led you to prepare.

The most effective leadership principle for you to embrace is *Only do what only you can do.*

That calls for prioritizing. If staff or volunteers can assume some of your responsibilities, delegate them and concentrate on the areas in which you excel. In your day planner, block out the non-negotiables (such as regular meetings, your children's activities, your sermon or lesson preparation, and your day off). Try not to take phone calls during the times you've blocked out, but be sure to return calls promptly.

Bob Shank serves as the program coordinator for all of the Franklin Graham Crusades. He is also the founder and president of The Master's Program. His ideas about time management are so practical. He suggests organizing your schedule into three types of days: Sabbath Days, Focus Days, and Buffer Days.

Sabbath Days are devoted to refreshment and renewal. They are purposeful days off dedicated to physical and spiritual rejuvenation.

Focus Days are scheduled in advance and designed for working on bold initiatives and visionary planning. The smallest block is a half day. Such days are most productive if you work off-site, away from your normal work setting. If that's not possible, turn the answering machine on, and put the "Do Not Disturb" sign on your door.

On Buffer Days you are accessible and undertaking normal daily tasks. You are interactive and chipping away at as many "in-box" tasks as possible. Bob Shank observes that the clergy is the group that has the hardest time taking Sabbath Days. We usually have five Buffer Days at work and two Buffer Days at home! I love the question he asks. How you answer it will determine how you handle the pressures of your day planner: "How could your life change if you had three Buffer Days and two Focus Days?"

Pressure From the Critics

I'm sure that some of the boaters that came alongside us were critical of our form or our boat's speed. Maybe they were thinking, *If we had that kind of boat, we could do that too.*

Even in the midst of a triumph some onlookers will look for the bad. Bill Cosby said, "I can't tell you what the key to success is, but I can tell you what the key to failure is—trying to please everyone."

Criticism is inevitable, but we need to fight the knee-jerk reaction to be defensive when we're criticized. First, evaluate the criticism. Is it just and accurate? Next, give the critic a fair hearing by listening to as much as he or she wants to share. Just keep saying, "Tell me more." This communicates that you really do value the feedback. (And remember, it's better to hear directly from your critics than having them telling everyone but you.) Finally, evaluate the validity of the criticism and, if necessary, apologize and make the necessary alterations.

Of course, in plenty of situations, criticism will be undeserved. Jesus went so far as to say, "Woe to you when all men speak well of you" (Luke 6:26). If we Christians are not *of* this world, then we can't seek the approval of everyone *in* this world. Several years ago a leader in our community called on the phone to announce that she was bringing a lawsuit against me for defamation of character. She'd heard that I had said something about her from the pulpit. Though I was caught off guard, I was able to say there had been no misrepresentation and I stood by my comments. While the conversation wasn't pleasant, with the Lord's help, I somehow was. The call ended after she said, "My lawyer will be in touch with you," and hung up.

While it cost me some sleep the next few nights, I knew my

statements were true and that I had the support of my leadership if the matter were to go to court. It didn't; she was merely crying wolf. As unpleasant as that experience was, it taught me two lessons. First, if you're a Christian leader, expect criticism from the world; it often confirms that you are exalting Christ. Second, learn to toughen up. Oswald Sanders says, "Maturity is moving from a thin skin and a hard heart to a thick skin and a soft heart."

Many local and national articles written about the ministry of Southeast Christian have been fair and balanced. Some haven't been fair at all! I recall one that made us out to be more concerned with money than ministry and more interested in statistics than the Spirit. Even after several visits and numerous interviews, I was unable to convince this poor reporter to take an objective look at what God was doing in our church. Here is a sample of his impressions of the preachers: "Both Russell and Stone are natural salesmen, with...easy smiles and the smooth ability to persuade an audience. There is no question that either could get rich selling ab-crunchers...on late-night infomercials."[1]

> ●
> # Expect criticism from the world; it often confirms that you are exalting Christ.

After reading his secular assessment of the preachers and the church, we thought it was obvious that he had missed the role the Holy Spirit plays in preaching and church growth. (We also knew that the author had never seen us with our shirts off!)

You can expect criticism from unbelievers, but some Christian leaders are surprised when criticism comes from within the Christian community. Jesus faced criticism from all sides, but his toughest critics were the religious leaders of the day—does that make you feel better about some of the problems you face? Church leaders get caught in the fray on all sorts of topics. Music styles in the church is one of the most volatile. If you want to experience pressure from critics, just introduce contemporary music to a traditional church service.

Sadly, parachurch organizations and churches will always have those who seek to make your ministry miserable. You teach, and they fold their arms. You tell a joke, and they roll their eyes. They derive fulfillment from pointing out your flaws and second-guessing your decisions. Someone has said, "The only thing more contagious than enthusiasm is the lack of it."

Expect the occasional anonymous note, the coward's way of confrontation. Dwight Moody once received an anonymous note that simply said, "Fool." Moody said, "It is the only time I ever received a letter where the person signed his name, but left off the message!" Critics are one more reason Christian leaders should stay put rather than change ministries every few years. The longer you stay, the more respect you earn and the more critics you outlast.

Conversely, changing ministries frequently merely requires you to re-encounter the same problems and struggles; only the names and faces have changed. Recently I told a politician weathering a vicious character attack to take solace in the fact that if we're getting shot at from behind, then we must truly be out in front! David Wheeler, a professor at Johnson Bible College, sometimes concludes his letters to those in ministry with these words: "May you have the heart of a child, the mind of a scholar, and the skin of a rhino."

Pressure From the Sponges

Another aspect of the "spotlight syndrome" is that churches and Christian organizations can become magnets for the needy. The spotlight is on us, the people see it, and they are drawn to us. Our purpose is to shepherd the flock and to take care of the truly needy, but the greater our influence, the more "sponges" we attract.

Let me explain what I mean by *sponges*...

There are people who just enjoy being close to Christian leaders; it feeds their egos and serves to improve their perception of their spirituality. Some want to be your best buddy. Others feel "you are the only one" who can help them. When you hear those words, alarms should go off in your brain. (If you grew up watching the television program *Lost in Space* in the late sixties, you may recall the robot saying, "Danger, Will Robinson!" That's the idea here.) When a person says, "I have to talk to you," have a strategy in place to help that individual. It may be through volunteers, referrals, another staff person, or a rare appointment with you.

Years ago I heard John Maxwell challenge Christian leaders to spend 80 percent of their time with the influencers and 20 percent of their time with non-influencers. Within the context of the lecture, he wasn't advocating favoritism, nor was he abdicating Jesus' challenge to do for "the least of these brothers of mine" (see Matthew 25:40). In fact, Jesus himself modeled this for us. While he taught us not to be too busy to be good Samaritans, he also withdrew from the crowds to be alone. Often he invested hours alone with three special disciples—Peter, James, and John. You see, the person who is *always* available isn't worth much when he *is* available!

> You see, the person who is *always* available isn't worth much when he *is* available!

Maxwell's words challenged me to be intentional and deliberate in planning time with leaders; otherwise, my time will be dominated by the sponges. When you put a sponge in a bucket of water, it knows its job. A sponge will soak up as much as it possibly can. If your phone messages follow a recurring theme, month after month, and the same people are "in crisis," time after time, then you are no doubt letting the sponges *sap* you rather than allowing the influencers to *stretch* you. You'll soon find yourself so drained that you have no energy to do the things that only you can do.

Leaders, be prepared for the pull on you. Recently a friend who runs a youth organization confirmed this warning. One of Paul's board members, an attorney, set up a lunch appointment with him. The two men ordered their food and made small talk until, about halfway through the meal, Paul bluntly asked, "So what do you need from me?"

The attorney said, "Paul, I don't need anything. I just wanted to spend some time with you."

Paul told me, "Those words caught me so off guard that I began to cry. It was so unexpected and refreshing that I sat there and just wept in the middle of this restaurant."

You see, Paul had been in the daily habit of receiving an unlimited number of people asking for help. Lunchtime had become a "sponge bath" for those in need of something. They were constantly sapping him, and the routine was slowly draining his energy and vision.

Young leaders may not understand Paul's story. Others of you may relate to it; you might even fantasize about a time when a person requesting an appointment says, "This will only take fifteen minutes"—and then it takes only fifteen minutes. Or a gift with no strings attached. A meal with no request for your help. A board meeting without an undertone of sarcasm.

On the other hand, as Colin Powell says, "The day people stop bringing you their problems is the day you have stopped leading them. They've either lost confidence or concluded you don't care." Of course we must remember our calling to care for people. We must balance our mandate to reach out to others with our need for legitimate personal boundaries. While we can prepare to

Learn to delegate and to say no.

avoid the sponges when kingdom work demands it, we must also remain willing to minister to them. Be Christlike and help people; Christian leaders should err on the side of compassion. But learn to delegate and to say no. And remember, there is something worse than being surrounded by people who are always trying to draw from your influence; it's when no one ever calls on you for help.

Pressure From the Resisters

The people taking pictures of us on our ski journey didn't realize that they had become a barrier. We couldn't turn because they

KEEPING YOUR HEAD ABOVE WATER

were alongside us. Even though the lake was wide enough, it was impossible to turn with boats blocking the way.

All leaders know how tough it is to be met with resistance, whether it is intentional or accidental. The plan is ready to unfold, and then barriers start popping up all over the place. Dee Hock, founder of Visa, says, "People don't resist change—people resist *being changed.*" Do you agree?

I heard about a New York lawyer who went duck hunting in rural Tennessee. He shot and dropped a bird, but it fell into a farmer's field on the other side of the fence. As the lawyer climbed over the fence, an elderly farmer drove up on his tractor and asked him what he was doing.

"I shot this duck, and it fell in this field, and now I'm going in to retrieve it."

"This is my property," the old farmer replied. "And you are not coming over here."

"I'm one of the best trial lawyers in New York, and if you don't let me get that duck, I'll sue you and take everything you own."

"Apparently, you don't know how we do things in these parts of Tennessee," said the farmer. "We settle disagreements like this with the Tennessee three-kick rule."

"And just what is the Tennessee three-kick rule?"

"Well, first I kick you three times, and then you kick me three times, and so on, back and forth, until someone gives up."

The attorney quickly thought about the proposed contest and decided that he could easily take the old-timer. He agreed to the local custom. The old farmer slowly climbed down from the tractor and walked up to the city slicker. His first kick planted the steel toe of his heavy work boot in the lawyer's shin. The man fell to his knees. His second kick nearly put a hole in the man's stomach. The old man then quickly delivered the third kick to the side of the attorney's head. Slowly, the disoriented lawyer managed to get to his feet.

"OK, you old codger," he said. "Now it's my turn."

The farmer smiled and said, "Naw, I give up. You can have the duck."

We Christian leaders can win the battle but lose the war.

My friend, we Christian leaders can win the battle but lose the war. Have you ever faced a situation in which, in order to win, you would lose a whole lot? In those cases you have to determine whether the cure is costlier than the disease. In other words, before taking on the resisters, be convinced that the result you are seeking is worth the price you will have to pay.

Leaders face these challenges every day. For example, a desire to grow may require decisions that cause a temporary dip in attendance or donations. David Novak is one of our church members at Southeast. He is better known as the CEO of Tricon Global Restaurants—Pizza Hut, Taco Bell, and KFC. David says, "Every decision a leader makes is a decision between pain and pleasure. We choose that which we think will bring us the most pleasure. We resist that, which in the end, we think will bring us the most pain. If you are standing on a burning ship, and the water is forty degrees, there comes a point when jumping in will allow you to feel better. But only briefly."

Laboring for the Lord entails making countless choices between pain and pleasure. Often our decisions bring changes by which someone gains something while someone else loses something.

In at least one respect, you are no different from the people you lead. To some degree, change is difficult for you, as well. While you may adamantly promote the idea of changing worship times, you may find it difficult to accept that the garbage at your home will be picked up on Wednesday morning this week instead of Monday. Routines are hard to change, but if you embrace and communicate the overall value of a particular change, pressures from the resisters will subside over time.

Change merely for the sake of change accomplishes nothing, though. There must be a purpose behind change in order to inform and convince the resisters. That's because at the root of resistance is uncertainty. Author and futurist Marilyn Ferguson said, "It's not so much that we are afraid of change or so in love with the old ways, but it's that place in between that we fear. It's like being between trapezes. It's Linus when his blanket is in the dryer; there's nothing to hold on to."

If you want to grow a church, you will face resistance. Those who are resistant to change usually buy into the idea of "Us Four and No More." They like being a big fish in a small pond. But Jesus said, "I, when I am lifted up from the earth, will draw all men to myself" (John 12:32). When Christ is glorified, he promises to attract people to himself. But entering stage right are the resisters. (When it comes to church growth, they pursue the Bonsai Method. You may recall the movie *The Karate Kid*. Master karate instructor Mr. Miyagi was always busy pruning, shaping, and trimming those miniature trees, the bonsai trees. The idea was "Keep it as small as you can without killing it!")

The pressure to survive rather than thrive flies in the face of healthy change. M.L. Hillard, a vice president with The ServiceMaster Company, says, "Change is an ocean; it will always be moving, slapping its boundaries. It will mock any attempt to contain it." Churches are notorious for resisting that ocean, but as long as they are contemplating healthy changes that don't compromise God's Word, they are wise to make the changes sooner rather than later. The Apostle Paul said, "I have become all things to all men so that by all possible means I might save some" (1 Corinthians 9:22).

Dave Dravecky was a great pitcher for the San Francisco Giants, but he was diagnosed with cancer and had to have his pitching arm and shoulder removed. A few years after that, I had the privilege of speaking on the same program as Dave. His attitude backstage really ministered to me. He saw his adversity as a chance to grow spiritually. He said to me, "Have you ever noticed that at the top of the mountains the trees are sparse and it's kind of brown and barren? But in the valleys you always find lush vegetation. In the valleys of life is where most of our growth occurs."

I've found his words to be true throughout my ministry. God has used the leadership challenges that I feel I can't handle to grow and deepen me. Pressure can be good. Most of us don't change when we see the light; we change when we feel the heat.

If you have a hard time dealing with pressure, then pay attention to Angela Thomas Guffey. She wrote these words after struggling with her ministry as a mom. Angela writes:

"Mothering requires everything. But eventually, everything given *plus* little replenished *equals* desperately empty. I held the empty cup of my soul out to my husband and begged him to fill it. I held out my cup to a bigger house and a minivan. But only Jesus could fill my soul. I tried my children and my girlfriends, but again, they could not fill the place designed by God for Himself.

"I had been mistaken. I thought that the goal of motherhood was to be a supermom. But in fact, the goal of mothering is to be a woman of God to your children. A woman of God is intimately connected to her Savior. A woman of God can love and give from the overflowing cup God has filled."[2]

Moms and ministers have a lot in common. They both have jobs that are never done, they are often overlooked, and they work with folks who are growing—and some who are babies!

The pressures of ministry can leave us feeling empty if we don't allow the Lord to regularly *fill our cup.*

The more pressures I encounter and the longer I lead, the more I have found that activity, attendance figures, and attention from "the boats alongside" cannot fill my cup. Only God can. Throughout this book you will notice a recurring theme: the importance of prayer. It is the fuel that carries you around the lake and throughout a lifetime of leadership. This chapter began with an observation that *leadership* is always accompanied by *pressure*. But there is another twosome that must travel together. *Pressure* should always be accompanied by *prayer*. Sometimes prayer changes things; usually prayer changes us. Without prayer the pressures of ministry can drown you, but with it "all things are possible."

For Group Discussion

1. When have you felt the most pressure from the spotlight? How did you respond?

2. What is the most difficult aspect of drawing personal boundaries in the face of constant need?

3. When have you said yes when you should have said no? What happened?

4. What are the unique pressures facing your church at the moment? From reading this chapter, what new insights have you gained about these situations? How might God be calling you to respond?

CHAPTER SIX

Teamwork in Leadership

Change is challenging and grueling. *What, you ask, could transform this collection of ten individuals into a team? The answer: making a turn and heading in the opposite direction. What makes the group turn so difficult is the mathematical reality that everyone is traveling at a different speed. It quickly became apparent that turning takes teamwork.*

❖ ❖ ❖ ❖ ❖ ❖

When the waters are rough and a change of direction is required, you quickly realize the need for a team effort. A collection of individuals, each of whom is looking out for number one, won't survive turns like these. That's why thriving organizations are committed to moving everyone in the same direction, regardless of the cost or consequences. Some may disagree with the process or the plan, but there comes a time when everyone must buy in. Teamwork is accelerated when you burn your bridges and everyone is committed to the cause.

We live in an era of transition. In the midst of quick changes of direction in the church and in business, teamwork is even more important. How can today's Christian leader foster teamwork? Let's explore several important requirements for effective teamwork in a church or another Christian organization.

Requirement 1: Recruit Diverse People

Selecting the team is almost as important as choosing the leader. Teamwork is important, but don't misunderstand me; you still need quality people with a strong leader who brings the team together. Bob Shank says, "Ignorance to the twelfth power does not become leadership." He's right. You could bring a bunch of duds together, who all get along, and have no leadership at all!

And a humble church leader surrounded by variously gifted individuals will always beat a talented, egotistical Lone Ranger over the long haul. So when you assemble your team, look for volunteers or staff members who are strong in areas in which you are weak. Part of the reason for the disciples' success in conveying the gospel message was just this type of diversity.

Christ assembled a diverse group that brought a wide range of gifts to the table. Matthew's position as a despised tax collector gave him a connection with lost, worldly people. Andrew's humility modeled the truth that knowing Jesus is more important than being known. Living in the shadow of his brother, Simon Peter, didn't prevent him from being a team player. James and John were the renegades. Knowing their rebellious natures, you probably wouldn't trust them if they volunteered to serve in your church parking lot. But Jesus picked these two to proclaim the good news. Jesus always sees people for *who they can become* rather than for who they are.

What goes through your own mind when you're looking for servant leaders to fill positions? When I need to add to our team at church, I put "a servant's heart" at the top of my list of requirements. Faithfulness to the mission of the organization is a close second. Of course, I look for God-given gifts in the area of our specific needs as well.

Early in my ministry I was interviewed for a position at a church in Illinois. I will never forget the final question I was asked by the senior pastor: "Is there anything or anyone that you love more than Jesus?"

"No," I said. Then I honestly added, "But a lot of times I allow him to slip into second or third place."

> •
> ## Jesus always sees people for *who they can become* rather than for who they are.

What a great question for any potential leadership team member to consider! Jesus said, "Where your treasure is, there your heart will be also" (Matthew 6:21). When assembling your leadership team, look for gifts that are distinctive, but remember that a passion for Christ should be the common denominator.

Many Christian leaders fall prey to the "mirror syndrome"—hiring or enlisting people with personalities similar to their own. Be sure to evaluate carefully. You may be subliminally drawn to individuals because they remind you of yourself. By hiring them you may duplicate your gifts rather than gain new ones that complement your own. Diversity and variety help to cover all the bases.

H.S. Vigeveno's book *13 Men Who Changed the World* includes a chapter dealing with Andrew. The title of the chapter is "He Used What He Had." This reminds me of a time I preached a revival in Mississippi. On the first day, only one person showed up to pray for the revival with the evangelist. His name was Sidney, and he was about forty years old. He was developmentally disabled, walked with a profound limp, and could barely speak intelligibly. But Sidney loved to pray and to serve.

I stayed next door at the preacher's house. Each night I would sit out on the front porch and look over my sermon, and about thirty minutes before the service, I would hear the distinctive sound of Sidney entering the church. He would limp up the front steps, unlock all the doors, and go around to turn on all the lights. Each

KEEPING YOUR HEAD ABOVE WATER

night, after the service was over and everyone had left, he made his way around the sanctuary, turning off the lights and locking the doors. Then he would head home until the next service.

I can't tell you how much that man's example touched me. Somebody might say, "He really didn't do that much." On the contrary, he did all that he could. Like Andrew, he used what he had. Whenever I hear a sermon on servanthood, I think about Sidney. I have a strong feeling that I'll get to see him again. When we're at heaven's door waiting to go in, I think God may say, "Hey, Sidney, would you help me open these gates and turn on the lights?" It really doesn't matter if you assemble a group of five-talent individuals or several one-talent or two-talent people. What matters is that, whatever talents they have, whether they're small or great, they lay them at the feet of Jesus.

The Lord can use any of us to help grow his church. So remember that diversity and teamwork go hand in hand.

Requirement 2: Communicate the Plan

Our water-skiing leader had to tell us what he had in mind for us to do. When ten skiers are following the same boat, the driver is the leader by default. Where he leads, we will follow. We appreciated his wisdom and thoughtfulness in communicating his plan to all of us through sign language. You see, many a good plan has bitten the dust because it wasn't effectively communicated. Leaders can't expect others to read their minds or to have long-term recall of a plan they previously unveiled. There must be an opportunity for give and take.

"Over-communication" and an excellent listening ear are two attributes of a great leader. Recently my kindergarten-age son came home and burst into tears. He told us he had gotten into trouble before school started for something he didn't do. My wife, Beth, asked him, "Samuel, did you try to explain to the teacher what you were doing?"

He said, "I tried, but she wouldn't let me explain." My son

learned at a young age how all of us feel when our voices aren't heard. If our opinions don't seem important to those in power, our lives can be very frustrating.

We've all been there, and Samuel will face the problem numerous times throughout his lifetime. Leaders must not forget how it feels to be left out or to have no input. This may seem obvious, yet, if assured confidentiality, many church staff members and volunteers would emphatically state that they have been left out of the loop. They don't feel privy to what others know. Whether they really *are* being excluded isn't the issue; if they *feel* left out of the process, we need to find ways to make them feel included.

Like it or not, perception is reality. If communication isn't perceived to be flowing to every team member, then the entire group will begin to sink. This is true for volunteers as well as lay leaders. Volunteers must know they are on the inside and be given as much information as possible so they can fulfill their particular responsibilities.

Try to set up channels that will facilitate communication—an e-mail reporting on the board meeting, a weekly meeting, or an open appointment at the same time each week, for example. Information is empowering. Talk to your staff and volunteers on a regular basis. Keeping them informed shows that you trust them and have confidence in them.

In fact, the number one complaint of both the staff and volunteers in any church or organization may be a lack of communication. Those *in the know* are often oblivious to the fact that those outside the circle want feedback. Those "outsiders" may feel they aren't given a chance to share their opinions. And *the perception of ostracism always leads to division.* You know you're in trouble when you hear statements such as these:

"I never know what's going on around here."

"They don't even bother to get our input anymore."

"It's so embarrassing when I hear things from my volunteers that no one bothered to tell me."

No one is exempt from being uninformed at one time or another.

Toughen up if that offends you; there is no getting around it. The goal, though, is to arrange for informative communication to be the norm rather than the exception. I must admit that this is not my forte. It has taken me years to realize that I may devise an excellent plan, but if I don't share it with my team—regularly, and in great detail—it's impossible for them to embrace it.

Err on the side of more communication, not less. (Do not confuse this with micromanagement, by which you suffocate your staff or volunteers by constantly looking over their shoulders.) Inclusion goes a long way toward building a team, because the knowledge of basic, everyday, nonconfidential information helps establish rock-solid loyalty. John Maxwell says, "I'm convinced that the surest way to establish a sense of ownership among your constituency is to involve them in the creative process, all along the

Err on the side of more communication, not less.

way. You might be able to reach a goal faster on your own, but when you get there you will be just that—on your own. Slow down, and take your people along."[1]

The driver of our boat believed in this principle. He made certain that every skier saw the signal that we were going to turn around. He knew that if just one of us missed the signal as he started this turn, it could be dangerous for the whole team.

Be certain that your co-laborers understand how you communicate. For example, as we added more women to our staff, we realized we had to alter the tenor of our staff meetings. Our guys bonded by picking on one another and by hurling heavy doses of sarcasm across the room. The women on our staff felt that the men were too brutal with one another. (Now we've struck a happy medium—we just pick on the women. *Not!*) For the sake of teamwork and unity in the body of Christ we have eased up. Through time and reflection, we've learned that we probably did cross the line of good-natured kidding and that, as a result, teamwork was not enhanced.

The driver of our boat clearly communicated that we were

heading for a major transition. He gave us sufficient warning, a chance to prepare, and an opportunity to brace for the worst. The Christian leader who wants effective teamwork will extend the same courtesy. He'll share his vision and plans rather than attempt to force them through. His ideas will be refined by the experience and wisdom of others. As a result, the entire team will get the credit. And if this group is truly God-honoring, the Lord will receive the glory.

Requirement 3: Encourage the Participants

Freely given encouragement breathes life into individuals and organizations. You might be surprised that the recipient of your encouraging voice mail messages listens to those messages again and again. Stop by someone's cubicle and you may see a thank you note prominently displayed, a little message you scribbled three weeks ago with little thought. I dare you to block out twenty minutes a week simply to encourage your team members! The benefits will astound you.

All of these seemingly insignificant acts of encouragement help create an environment in which teamwork flourishes. That teamwork is so important when you face a radical change of direction. Just as it did with my water-skiing buddies, a sincere high five goes a long way with your staff and volunteers. Successful leaders don't resemble dictators. Russell H. Ewing said, "A boss creates fear, a leader confidence. A boss fixes blame, a leader corrects mistakes. A boss knows all, a leader asks questions. A boss makes work drudgery, a leader makes it interesting. A boss is interested in himself or herself, a leader is interested in the group."[2]

In fact, the leader's responsibility is not to police the masses, looking for mistakes. Rather, good leaders create an environment in which people have the latitude to suggest different methods and to think outside the box. If an idea fails, it fails—but it's important that team members have the freedom to fail and to learn from the experience.

I heard of a teenager whose first job was working as a delivery boy for a florist. One day the boy was to deliver two sets of flowers. One set was for a funeral home, and the other was for a big church that had relocated to a larger sanctuary.

The florist knew there was a problem when he received a phone call from an irate minister. The preacher said, "We've got a beautiful new sanctuary with a basket of flowers up front that says, 'Rest in Peace.' "

"You think *you've* got problems!" the florist replied. "Somewhere in this city there's a nice bouquet of flowers sitting beside a casket with a sign that says, 'Good luck in your new location!' "[3]

Allow your team members to make mistakes, and encourage them to learn from those mistakes.

Encourage the creativity of your staff and volunteers by giving them opportunities to brainstorm and "mindmap." Look for ways to add to your ministry's effectiveness rather than merely continuing the same old programs year in and year out. This is what leadership guru Jim Collins refers to as "the genius of the 'and,' rather than the tyranny of the 'or.' "

Encouragement can be given publicly or privately. Both types are needed. Type A personalities long for public encouragement. Type B personalities appreciate encouragement more if it's given privately. But regardless of a teammate's temperament, either type of praise is appreciated and essential for building a team.

Part of the benefit that flows from special projects and events is the appreciation you gain for other ministries and volunteers.

Praise is appreciated and essential for building a team.

For example, when Bible-college students spent the weekend at our church for a ministry conference I directed, the women's circles provided housing for them. I was encouraged by their hospitality. When the Fellowship of Christian Athletes held a fund-raising auction, the student leaders stepped up to the plate. I was encouraged by their attention to details and gift of administration. When our church put together a "friend weekend," the members of our children's ministries department took ownership of the event as if it were their own. I was encouraged by their creativity and desire to promote the weekend to all ages. When our church presents an Easter pageant or a Christmas program, I am always encouraged by the servants' hearts of the members of the facilities team. They go beyond the call of duty, working late on behalf of the other ministries and Christ.

So no matter how busy you are, always remember that navigating the rough waters requires an occasional boost of encouragement. Take time to give it in large doses.

Requirement 4: Instill Unity of Purpose

As we were skiing, we got close to one another, but we were careful not to step on one another. The Apostle Paul knew that a division among Christians is a poor witness that can paralyze the power of the church. The size of the ministry doesn't matter; division is just as deadly in a church of eighty as it is in a church of eight thousand. Paul minces no words when he says, "Make every effort to keep the unity of the Spirit through the bond of peace" (Ephesians 4:3). In other words, *don't step on others*.

When 180-degree changes loom ahead, stick together and hold on. Remind others *why* you are doing *what* you are doing. Tie the change in with your mission or vision statement. In Romans 12:18 Paul says, "If it is possible, as far as it depends on you, live at peace with everyone." Paul went to great pains to encourage teamwork within the body of believers. But the apostle also left the door open since, in rare cases, unity of purpose may be impossible.

> When 180-degree changes loom ahead, stick together and hold on.

Do your best, but realize that in some situations people may need to be released from certain responsibilities and redirected to areas in which harmony comes more naturally. Those times are stressful, but I've found that, in the long run, such prayerfully considered decisions have been vindicated. It may take such a measure to improve the teamwork of the whole organization.

Because you work in a church or a parachurch organization doesn't mean that relationships will always be peaches and cream. Personality conflicts will arise; contrasting styles won't always mesh. Someone has put it this way:

"To live above with the saints I love,

Oh, that will be glory!

But to dwell below,

With the saints I know—

Now that's a different story!"

Decide early in your ministry that you will not allow Satan to divide your staff members or volunteers. A lost world desperately needs the message of Christ. Your team must model his love and spirit of unity.

Finally, I must remind you that some leaders seek name recognition or personal glory, and that's a devastating barrier to unity. Others, though, have a genuine kingdom consciousness. They care about their staff members. They treat their volunteers with respect. Those leaders have the big picture in mind, so they set their sights on building a true team. Banker Walter Wriston, who writes for the *Harvard Business Review*, says, "The person who figures out how to harness the collective genius of the people in his or her organization is going to blow the competition away!"[4]

This idea goes deeper than just spending time together as co-laborers, because there's a difference between "union" and "unity." If you tie two cats together by their tails you will have union—but you probably won't have unity. True Christian unity is based upon being "in Christ," sharing together in the life of the Son who dwells in all of you. That's more than a social relationship, and it goes even deeper than a spirit of camaraderie or even deep friendship. So after assembling your team and communicating the plan, you must aim the members of your team in the direction of their main purpose, which is to bring glory to their Savior.

With Teamwork, It's Possible!

I've never lifted a barn, but Herman Ostry, a farmer in Bruno, Nebraska, has. Shortly after buying a piece of land with a barn on it, he watched as a nearby creek rose until twenty-nine inches of water ran through the barn. He half-jokingly said to his family, "I bet if we had enough people, we could pick up that barn and carry it to higher ground."

His son Mike did some calculating. He figured that the barn weighed about nineteen thousand pounds. If each person lifted about fifty-five pounds, it would take only 344 people to carry the barn to higher ground. Mike then went on to design a grid of steel tubing and attach it to the inside of the barn. Next he put handles all around the outside of this grid. On July 30, 1988, the day the town of Bruno celebrated its centennial, 344 people took their places at those handles. As thousands watched, Herman Ostry counted, "One, two, three..." The barn was lifted. A crowd cheered as the lifters carried that nine-ton barn fifty yards up a hill in just three minutes.

How did they do it? Teamwork.

They gathered enough people to work toward a common goal and spread the load evenly. Then—with one heart, one mind, one purpose, one direction—they were able to accomplish the seemingly impossible. When we called to check the accuracy of this story, Mrs. Ostry confirmed it, but she said we omitted one major detail. She said, "Not only did they move it, but they also *turned the barn.*"

Because of my water-skiing experience, I was impressed by this additional detail. In fact, anyone who has led others through a major change can understand why Mrs. Ostry felt it was important to add this detail. The lesson is clear. It doesn't matter whether you are 344 "barn raisers," ten skiers, or a church staff of four. If you want to move in a new direction, you know that *turning takes teamwork.*

Several years ago, at the Calgary Stampede in Canada, something unusual happened during a pulling contest. This particular contest is designed to determine which horse can pull the greatest weight. The winning horse pulled a little *over* nine thousand pounds, while the second-place horse managed to drag a little *under* nine thousand pounds. Afterward, the two owners decided to give the crowd a demonstration of teamwork. They harnessed the two horses to see how much they could pull together. To the crowd's surprise, it wasn't eighteen thousand pounds. It was twenty-seven thousand!

What a lesson for the onlookers! Teamwork allows us to accomplish so much more than we might ever dream possible. There *is* strength in numbers. When you run smack-dab into a wave that you yourself may have helped create, know that you are not alone. And know that it is better to have a rough ride through the transitions—as a team—than to sink slowly in defeat.

For Group Discussion

1. What key principle or point in this chapter rang a bell with you? Why?

2. How diverse would you say your church's leadership teams are? What could bring more diversity in the future? Is this an important goal for your church or organization? Why or why not?

3. What are some of the most common ways leaders fail to communicate?

4. What are some of the most effective ways leaders communicate in your own church or organization? What new methods could be implemented?

5. When has someone encouraged you in your ministry? How did that feel? When have you encouraged another in ministry? What good effects flowed from your action?

6. Describe the degree of unity of purpose among your team members. How did you and the team arrive at this level? How could you achieve a greater degree of unity and genuine Christian fellowship?

CHAPTER SEVEN

Faithfulness in Leadership

If I could finish strong, the pain would be worth it.

There was no denying my exhaustion. My legs felt like jelly; my arms were like taut rubber bands. Yet I knew our achievement was about to be recognized and applauded. We'd entered the final quarter mile, the homestretch. Family and friends whom we'd deserted ten minutes ago were now coming into sight. Our accomplishment would become the small talk at summer parties and announced during conversation lulls at family reunions.

Surely I could remain faithful to the end.

❖ ❖ ❖ ❖ ❖ ❖

Many Christian leaders have begun their ministries with patience, balance, teamwork, and the ability to handle pressure, and they've cruised along just fine until their world came crashing down. The failure may or may not have been self-imposed. But whether the outward cause was a power-hungry team member within a church, a declining donor base in a parachurch organization, or even a personal moral failure, in the final analysis the real cause is usually some form of breakdown in faithfulness.

I've replayed the scene of my water-skiing fall countless times in my mind (even though my competitive nature makes it very frustrating to even think about it!). It was the best of times and the worst of times; I experienced the thrill of victory and the agony of defeat. The simplest explanation is that I was so excited that I dropped my guard and loosened my grip. Instead of allowing my knees to absorb the bounce of the big wave, I tensed up and crashed like a rookie. *Next time* you can bet I'll be faithful to the end.

I know a minister who pastored a church of two thousand members back in the 1980s. Then this minister had an adulterous affair. He later told me that he would choose to lose both of his legs if he could relive that time and remain pure and faithful to his wife and to the Lord. Sadly, this is not an isolated event. It seems to me that faithfulness isn't as popular as it should be among Christian leaders. Presidents and preachers drop their guard (and some even their trousers), and in the process they lose their reputations. Through counseling, repentance, and a change of behavior they may rebound from their fall, but the scars remain.

Christian businessman Bob Shank served as a pastor for a few years before joining a group of preachers who got together for mutual accountability and sermon preparation. One of the men in the group half-jokingly said, "Bob, welcome to the profession where, if you stay married to your wife and keep your nose clean, in ten years you'll be in the top 10 percent." The line would be more humorous if it didn't have so much truth in it.

Faithful to Your Vow to the Lord

When I put on my water skis and took hold of the tow rope, my bridges were burned. I had decided to follow the boat; there was no turning back. I couldn't think, *I'll see how this goes for a while, and then maybe I'll quit.* That just wasn't an option. My decision had been made as soon as the question "Do you have someone who is willing to go?" was asked. My splash into the water two seconds later was the answer. But what, exactly, will it mean for you to remain faithful to the Lord in your ministry? Let me suggest a few possibilities...

1. Faithfulness may simply mean "hanging in there." I love the title of one of Eugene Peterson's books: *A Long Obedience in the Same Direction*. It reminds us that when we accepted Jesus as the Lord of our lives, we were vowing to faithfully follow him forever out of gratitude for his pure grace. It reminds me of the nickname Greg Allen (our worship leader at Southeast) and I use for each other: Long-Haulers. The nickname reinforces what we committed to each other years ago: to serve together at this church for the *long haul*.

There will be times you'll be tempted to throw in the towel. Selling cars might provide more money, and perhaps produce less stress, than trying to minister to people. But don't be hasty. Cavitt Roberts said, "Maturity is the ability to stay with a resolution, long after the mood in which the resolution was made has left." Remember your calling, and hold tightly to the tow rope.

> •
> **Remember your calling, and hold tightly to the tow rope.**

2. Faithfulness often means a willingness to be bored or underutilized, at least for a while. Certain aspects of your ministry will be more enjoyable than others. Every career package contains a few undesirable responsibilities. John Bradley and Jay Carty, in their video series *Unlocking Your Sixth Suitcase*, speak of the "sixty-forty principle." If you remember it, your ministry will likely last for the long haul. They say, "The best you can realistically expect for your work is that 60 percent of your time will be spent on tasks that draw on your natural talent strengths. This means that 40 percent of your time at work can consist of boredom, routine, red-tape, maintenance, clean-up, and hassle. If you can develop the perspective that 60 percent is about as good as it's going to get, then you can relax without getting caught up in an unrealistic search for a big payoff."[1]

My Mondays are filled with meetings. The way I'm wired, I find that those meetings make up a big part of the "less desirable" 40 percent. For more than an hour every Monday morning, the Preaching and Worship Ministries group evaluates the previous weekend's services. We also peruse the components of the upcoming Wednesday and weekend services. Then Bob or I talk about next week's sermon. Some brainstorming follows.

Next on the agenda is a two- to three-hour meeting with six other ministers and our senior administrator. In this meeting we delve into the overall ministry. The day is usually rounded out with a committee meeting involving lay leaders and staff. Even though I love the people and am passionate about the topics we discuss, six hours of meetings is still six hours of meetings. I am thankful that those vital meetings are not more than 40 percent of my responsibilities. *Make certain that the ministry path you pursue allows more than half of your time to utilize your primary gifts and core passions.*

Vanna White on *Wheel of Fortune* has a tough job. She gets paid a fortune herself for turning those letters. I would venture to guess that she enjoys the pay (and looking pretty), but I wonder if she enjoys clapping her hands approximately 720 times every half-hour! That has to be in the 40 percent (along with all the hours spent cramming, studying vowels and consonants!).

It is easy to procrastinate, putting off the parts of your job that you don't like, repeatedly transferring them to the next day's to-do list. But one challenge for the faithful is to put the less-desirable items at the top of the list. Deal with them first, and you can spend the rest of your day doing the things that you enjoy. Have you heard this saying? "If you have to swallow a frog, don't look at it very long. And if you have to swallow more than one, swallow the big ones first!" Learn that lesson early, and your ministry will be a blessing and not a curse.

KEEPING YOUR HEAD ABOVE WATER

3. Faithfulness should mean it's OK to be small.

The size of your ministry is ultimately up to God. Yes, he does want the church to grow—but in his way and time. A Faithfulness Hall of Fame, in my opinion, would be populated by people with long-term ministries in small-church settings whose goal is to grow God's kingdom without much personal recognition. These people serve with less hoopla; they lead fewer followers. They are forced to wear many different hats in addition to meeting their flocks' spiritual needs. That takes faithfulness—the faithfulness to be small at least for now. Such faithful ministers might have to mow the lawn, and their kids might help fold the church bulletins every Saturday. But they are faithful.

Faithful to the Work He Gives You

You are not going to enjoy every aspect of Christian leadership. But God didn't call you to be happy all the time; he called you to be faithful to the work.

Nancy, a Christian woman in our church, is one of those lay leaders who makes you wish cloning would be legalized. Recently I presented her with an award in front of our entire staff. For three years of her life she volunteered an average of about sixty hours a week to coordinate and lead the cleaning of our entire building. I gave her a gift and a hug and asked her to share a few words with the staff. With tears in her eyes, she said, "It's not about me; it's about him."

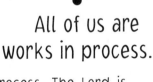

All of us are works in process.

Her index finger pointing upward could well have been sign language for the word *faithfulness*. All of us are works in process. The Lord is sharpening us and molding us into his image until the day we die.

Christian author and speaker Steve Farrar tells a story about three young evangelists who popped into the national spotlight in the 1950s. If you were to ask people then which of the three was the most talented and compelling speaker, the same two names would always be mentioned. But those two fell away from the Lord; one committed suicide, and the other got involved with alcohol and drugs. But the third now has a freeway named after him in North Carolina because people saw faithfulness and consistency through decades of ministry in the life of...Billy Graham.

Over time a person's true colors are revealed. Author John D. Beckett said, "Work is a high calling, not secondary in value...Work takes on added dignity as we regard each person we contact in business with great respect, and as we function in a framework of excellence and integrity. It is essential that our success never be at the expense of our soul—there is more to consider than the bottom line. The norms and values rooted in the Bible can serve as a compass in this regard, on seas that can be turbulent and treacherous."[2]

Faithful to Your Marriage Vows

Faithfulness involves staying true, not only to the Lord and his work, but also to your spouse. Years ago I heard a preacher on the radio say, "If you hear that I've had an affair with another woman, don't you believe it. I love my wife too much to ever break that vow." But while I love my wife and have every intention of remaining faithful to my marriage vows, I will never boast of my ability to do it. Oswald Chambers spoke of unguarded strengths becoming a double weakness. Paul warns us, "Watch yourself, or you also may be tempted" (Galatians 6:1).

We are all vulnerable to the withering attacks of lust. One thing I didn't mention in my skiing story was that the water-skier who fell first was one of the most talented of the group. He knew what he was doing; he was just looking in the wrong direction. Don't say it can't happen to you. It happened to the *strongest* man in the Bible, Samson. It happened to the *wisest* man in the Bible, Solomon. It happened to the *most spiritual* man in the Bible, David. And if it happened to them, it can certainly happen to you and to me.

Men are especially vulnerable in this area. One study showed that 95 percent of men struggle with lust. (I'd guess that the other 5 percent struggle with lying.) A Christian men's magazine

KEEPING YOUR HEAD ABOVE WATER

reports that 37 percent of pastors "admitted in a Christianity Today survey that they struggle with Internet pornography."[3]

All of this reminds me of the young man who asked the old priest, "Father, when will I be freed from the lust of the flesh?"

The priest replied, "I wouldn't trust myself until I'd been dead for three days."

The most spiritual among us can be the most vulnerable. Priest and author Henri Nouwen lends some insight here: "It is precisely the men and women who are dedicated to spiritual leadership who are easily subject to raw carnality. The reason for this is that they do not know how to live the truth of the Incarnation. They separate themselves from their own concrete community, try to deal with their needs by ignoring them or satisfying them in distant or anonymous places, and then experience an increasing split between their own most private inner world and the good news they announce. *When spirituality becomes spiritualization, life in the body becomes carnality.* When ministers and priests live their ministry mostly in their heads and relate to the Gospel as a set of valuable ideas to be announced, the body quickly takes revenge by screaming loudly for affection and intimacy."[4]

> The most spiritual among us can be the most vulnerable.

We must have a group of peers with whom we can share our deepest longings and talk about our most intense desires. The loneliness and pressures of ministry will drive us to seek escape, and we'll be tempted to find relief in the arms of another—or through unbridled fantasy.

I have a clipping that for the past seven years has been on my desk where only I can see it. It's a newspaper story about a local preacher who had an affair and lost his church. Believe it or not, the clipping is from USA Today. That yellowed piece of paper serves to remind me of the negative ripples that can spread across a nation if I drop my guard or if you drop your guard. The enemies of God will mock Christian leaders and Christ as well. If you ever want to destroy your family and your ministry—not to mention your reputation—have an affair or become entangled in pornography.

You see, Satan loves to try to get you to lose your equilibrium in the face of temptation. So be prepared; put up hedges of protection. For example, I have a window in my office door. This serves to protect me from false charges and to prevent me from becoming too casual in conversations with women. Here are other safeguards that may prevent you from falling.

Safeguard 1: Avoid creating a setting for sin. It's so easy to create an enticing situation. For instance, do you ever travel alone in a car with a person of the opposite sex? Do you undertake long-term counseling with persons of the opposite sex? These people may always see you at the top of your game, when you look and act your best. A counselee who feels neglected at home might become attracted to you. And ongoing praise and affirmation from the lonely can feed more than just your ego.

The cause of a fall might be a sudden, unexpected wave of temptation, but usually it's something we can see coming and can take steps to avoid. Men are notorious for saying, "I can handle that relationship without it bringing me down." How arrogant we can be! It's like an alcoholic saying, "I can keep a beer in the refrigerator," or a men's accountability group meeting weekly at the local Hooters restaurant. Don't put out the welcome mat for sin.

> • Praise and affirmation from the lonely can feed more than just your ego.

Pride always comes before a fall. You may have helped create a sinful situation through your own flirtations or desire for attention; if so, you will be knocked down by your own doing. Let's make sure we aren't creating a setting for sin, where a powerful wave could be devastating. Paul Benjamin said, "It's easier to drift than to swim against the current."

Many Christians have penciled sin into their day planners! They plan their mischief and dalliances. They compartmentalize their secret lives and their ministry lives and begin to rot from the inside out. When that happens, it doesn't even take a big wave to bring them down; a perfectly timed ripple can cause the fall. Decide right now that you will not become another statistic, another Christian casualty who disgraces the cause of Christ.

Several years ago my accountability partner and I made lists of all the people who would be hurt if either of us were to be unfaithful to our wives. It was astounding; it also put the fear of the Lord in us. I encourage every Christian to do this exercise.

Safeguard 2: Learn—and practice—good running skills. How was Joseph able to withstand Potiphar's wife? How did he keep his balance in those rough waters? His response in the heat of the moment offers some insight into his relationship with his heavenly Father. Joseph declined the advances of this influential temptress, saying, "How could I do such a wicked thing and sin against God?" (Genesis 39:9). Joseph's love for God was so strong that the enticing pleasures of the flesh paled in comparison. How strong is your love for God?

Instead of giving in to temptation, Joseph ran. Now that doesn't sound terribly spiritual, but in order to walk with God, sometimes we must run from the devil. It seems in today's society we've lost our sense of the seriousness of sin, and we've forgotten that sin—especially sexual sin—wounds the heart of God. You may be thinking, *Oh, I thought sin was sin.* Yes it is; it is "missing the mark." But listen to what the Apostle Paul says: "Flee from sexual immorality. All other sins a man commits are outside his body, but he who sins sexually sins against his own body. Do you not know that your body is a temple of the Holy Spirit, who is in you, whom you have received from God? You are not your own; you were bought at a price. Therefore honor God with your body" (1 Corinthians 6:18-20).

Safeguard 3: Know, and stay aware of, your personal E.Q. (Enticement Quotient). Are you fully aware of your particular weaknesses in alluring situations, when you're tired, lonely, or bored? Can you state exactly which kinds of temptation cause you to be the most vulnerable? And are you always vigilant against these special enticements?

Several years ago, on New Years Eve, I pulled into my driveway at about 10 p.m. and saw a big, fat possum scurrying into my back yard. I was thrilled to see him because our garbage had been getting turned over for weeks and I'd been uncertain of the culprit. So I went inside and got a flashlight, along with my number 3 iron. (Since I have a hard time hitting a golf ball with it, I felt the odds were better that I could hit a possum!) After searching the back yard, I finally found him up in a tree trying to look inconspicuous. When I poked the iron in his direction, he assumed an attack position, exposed his fangs, and prepared to pounce on me. At this point I retreated inside to ponder another course of action.

> He'll just keep changing the menu until he finds something you can't resist.

The next day, I phoned my friend John, who lives on a farm. He gave me a cage in which to catch the little beast. Each night for a week I bundled up the kids and took them outside to sprinkle food along a trail leading to the cage and to check the trap.

After several days, I called John to tell him that my efforts had been unsuccessful. He asked, "Well, are you changing the menu?"

"What do you mean by that?"

"Try different foods," he said, "until you find something he really likes."

So one night we chose pizza for his entree, and the next morning we found pizza in the cage, but not outside. (By the way, he was a thin-crust lover.) Another night we had ground beef. Later we put ham on the menu, and early the next morning my wife, Beth, yelled, "We caught the possum!"

The whole family bundled up and went outside. We were so excited that we even took a family picture with the little critter. (There's not a lot to do in Kentucky.) As the story of the capture circulated within the church, people began asking me a simple question: "Is it hard to catch a possum?"

Each time I'd reply, "Not really—you just have to keep changing the menu until you finally find something he can't resist."

You know what? That is Satan's strategy for attempting to turn the faithful into the faithless. At first he entices you with someone's *appearance*. If that doesn't work, he may tempt you with someone's *affluence*. If that fails, he may try to have someone start giving you a lot of *attention*. Satan knows what he's doing. He'll just keep changing the menu until he finds something you can't resist.

Listen to the wisdom of a man who should have known more about women than anyone. Solomon warned, "With persuasive words she led him astray; she seduced him with her smooth talk. All at once he followed her like an ox going to the slaughter, like a deer stepping into a noose till an arrow pierces his liver, like a bird darting into a snare, little knowing it will cost him his life" (Proverbs 7:21-23).

Safeguard 4: Determine always to remain *one* person rather than *two*. Chris Dewelt is a professor of missions at Ozark Christian College in Joplin, Missouri. I once heard him speak at a convention, and I remember these powerful words: "I am to be the same person whether I'm holding a Communion tray in my hand or a remote control. I am to be the same person whether I'm in a hotel room five hundred miles from home or in the family room with my kids. I am to be the same person when I'm reading my Bible or browsing through a Barnes & Noble bookstore. I am to be the same person whether I'm on break at work or walking through the sanctuary of my church. For what matters is my integrity, my purity, and my faithfulness."

The author of the book of Hebrews challenged the early Christians by saying, "Let us fix our eyes on Jesus, the author and perfecter of our faith, who for the joy set before him endured the cross, scorning its shame, and sat down at the right hand of the throne of God" (Hebrews 12:2).

Faithful in *All* Things

Faithfulness must go beyond sexual purity, of course. While that is a good place to start, it's a poor place to finish. We need Christian leaders who are faithful in paying their bills in a timely fashion, for instance. God wants his representatives to value ministry over money, to remember their initial calling rather than the call of worldly success. He wants us to be faithful in all things, faithful in keeping our word, faithful in pursuing our vows, faithful in deepening our relationship with him. The Lord certainly set the example for us. Hebrews 10:23 says, "Let us hold unswervingly to the hope we profess, for he who promised is faithful."

George MacDonald put the matter in perspective when he said, "He who is faithful over a few things is a lord of cities. It does not matter whether you preach in Westminster Abbey, or teach a ragged class, so you be faithful. The faithfulness is all."[5]

> •
> The biblical view of faithfulness is a far cry from the world's description of success.

The biblical view of faithfulness is a far cry from the world's description of success. God's economy is different. He's not studying your church paper to see the size of your annual budget. His finger isn't busy counting heads while you preach. He focuses upon faithfulness, not numbers. At the same time, I believe he enjoys sending blessings—and people—where he sees faithfulness and sincerity. And just as with Christ's ministry, at times he wants us to be willing to leave the ninety-nine to faithfully minister to the one.

Robert McQuilkin was the president of Columbia Bible College and Seminary in South Carolina. After forty years of marriage, his wife, Muriel, became lost in the fog of Alzheimer's disease. The disease had progressed to the point that she would walk the mile from their home to her husband's office between five and ten times a day. Several years ago he retired in order to care for her. Here is what Robert McQuilkin said when he announced to the faculty and students that he was retiring early:

"Throughout my life I have experienced easy decision-making on major decisions. But one of the simplest and clearest decisions I've ever had to make is this one, because circumstances dictated it. Muriel, in the last couple of months, seems to be happy when with me, and almost never happy when not with me. In fact, when she can't get to me, she feels very trapped and fearful. But when I am with her, she is happy and contented.

"And so I must be with her at all times. You see, it's not only that I have promised in sickness and in health, until death do us part. I am a man of my word, but it is also the only fair thing to do. She sacrificed for me for forty years to make my ministry possible. So, if I cared for her for forty years I would still be in debt. However, it's not that I *have* to, but that I *get* to. I love her very dearly. She is a delight, and it is a great honor to get to care for such a wonderful person."

Sometimes a Christian leader steps away from the masses to keep his vow to one. Simply put, that is faithful leadership. And when you lead in that manner, you'll maintain your balance and avoid a fall, no matter how big the wave. That's the two-fold challenge for today's Christian leader: to keep your vow to one and to keep your vow to One.

What About the Failures?

Finally, let me say a word to anyone who has fallen and been doused with guilt and disappointment. You have probably experienced a variety of emotions because you know it takes years to rebuild a reputation.

But the Lord can do it.

Restoration and renewal can come through prayer, repentance, and time. God can still use you and, more important, God still loves you. He wants your repentance; he wants you to openly confess your mistake and come clean. He wants no finger-pointing and no prideful, defensive explanations of your actions; he simply wants to hear the honest, sincere declaration "I have sinned." He wants to reconcile you and, in his time, to restore you to some type of service. Your ministry may not be as visible or public as it was before, but his Spirit wants to mold you, make you, and conform you to his image.

The big spills in life are painful. Listen to David the adulterer's journey as described in Psalm 32:5: "Then I acknowledged my sin to you and did not cover up my iniquity. I said, 'I will confess my transgressions to the Lord'—and you forgave the guilt of my sin." Acknowledgement—confession—forgiveness—restoration. Notice that God doesn't just forgive the sin. He forgives the *guilt* of your sin. Wow! We all know too many stories of people who had been Christian leaders for decades and then were blindsided by a wave of lust or a ripple of riches. Their fall was hard and affected many others.

Sam Houston was the first president of the Republic of Texas. I've heard he was a rather nasty fellow with a checkered past. Later in life he made a commitment to Christ and was baptized in a river. The preacher said to him, "Sam, your sins are washed away."

Houston replied, "God help the fish."

While my skiing "baptism" was unintentional, it was similar to my spiritual baptism when I was a young man. Both were humbling, and both required me to admit my need for help. I realized that, by myself, I would continue to fall.

Tommy Nelson, in his lectures on the Song of Solomon, will sometimes tell church audiences, "If you knew about me what God knows about me—you wouldn't come in here to listen to me." He then goes on to say, "But if I knew about you what God knows about you, we wouldn't let you in! So it's all the same."

We all fall. We all have some skeletons in our closets that haunt us. Some skeletons are deeds, others are thoughts, but both indicate a fall below God's standard.

True leaders get up after a fall. And they seek to remain faithful to the One who helped them up.

KEEPING YOUR HEAD ABOVE WATER

For Group Discussion

1. Which of the three descriptions of faithfulness (pp. 91-93) had the greatest impact on you? Why?

2. Do you agree with Henri Nouwen that those who are the most dedicated to spiritual leadership can be the most tempted? Explain.

3. How alone are you in ministry? To what extent are you accountable to others?

4. What is your reaction to the safeguards suggested in this chapter? What other safeguards have you found helpful?

5. How would you counsel a younger person or a "rookie minister" in the area of faithfulness and temptation? What main points would you emphasize?

6. How do you typically handle your failings in faithfulness? What can you do to rely more upon God's grace and less upon your own willpower in the future?

CHAPTER EIGHT

Celebration of Leadership

We laughed and smiled and relished our ten-minute lap around the lake.

To my pleasant surprise, supportive relatives and friends were heaping praise on me with only an occasional veiled reference to my humiliating splashdown. Loved ones have seen plenty of my blunders, and one more wouldn't cause desertion. All they cared about was that I had done my best and made a memory that would last a lifetime.

As I shared my disappointment with them, I wasn't wanting their pity; rather, I was searching for acceptance. It was a gift they graciously gave me.

During the rest of the afternoon and evening, we celebrated the experience.

❖ ❖ ❖ ❖ ❖ ❖

We hear a great deal about patience, teamwork, and faithfulness. Seldom do we hear much about celebration. Celebrating seems to be a waste of time for the diligent Christian leader intent on saving a lost world.

You may have seen the chapter title and thought, *Why would Dave write about celebrating? The loser fell; he bit the dust; he took a dive.*

KEEPING YOUR HEAD ABOVE WATER

How right you are. I fell; I failed. But I agree with Charles Swindoll, who said, "Stumblers who, when they fall down, stay down, are a dime a dozen. In fact, they are useless. But stumblers who, when they fall down, get back up, are as rare as rubies; in fact, they're priceless."

In the midst of all the verbal replays of our ten-man skiing adventure, someone pointed out that *I had finished*. It just wasn't pretty. I'd give a lot to have had a spectacular ending—perhaps a massive wave could have knocked a ski off of one foot and, like a coordinated flamingo, I could have ridden out the final yards in an amazing display of skill and strength. Honestly, I wish that had happened. But we can't go back and unscramble eggs.

> **We can't go back and unscramble eggs.**

At least I finished, though.

The Bible is full of wounded leaders who found hope and grace in God after their failures, people whose journeys were marred but whose finishes honored God. Many church leaders, and some biblical characters, have fallen in the final hundred yards of their service to God. Lot was righteous enough that God saved him from death in Sodom, but later he got drunk and slept with his daughters. David, the man after God's own heart, committed adultery and had the husband murdered to cover the crime. These true stories are quite a bit less flattering than my watery demise. But like me, somehow David and Lot dog-paddled their way to the finish line.

As the Apostle Paul was completing his journey, he began his celebration with these words: "I have fought the good fight, I have finished the race, I have kept the faith. Now there is in store for me the crown of righteousness, which the Lord, the righteous Judge, will award to me on that day—and not only to me, but also to all who have longed for his appearing" (2 Timothy 4:7-8).

As long as you finish the race, your time doesn't disqualify you from the celebration. God is counting on you to complete the course and head for the celebration. In this chapter you'll discover four excellent reasons for Christian leaders to celebrate.

Celebrate the Victories

Historically, Christian organizations and churches are pretty lax when it comes to celebrating. Had my skiing partners been a group of ten Christian leaders, the celebration would have been scrapped and replaced by a meeting to determine how we could add anyone skiing in our general vicinity to our attendance count. A promotion committee would have been appointed to get the local paper to cover the story. Two skiers would have been sent to the closest McDonald's in the hope that Ronald and his crew would be willing to donate free orange drinks to the spectators. Christian leaders often feel too busy to take the time to revel in the blessings God has handed out. As a result they miss out on a wonderfully therapeutic way of acknowledging their accomplishments. The Jews used to set aside an entire year for celebration; all I'm lobbying for is an hour or two!

Even Scripture talks about celebrating. Paul anticipated the victor's crown at the end of the race. He envisioned God's people in a joyful, triumphant procession (2 Corinthians 2:14). Yet we Christians do shy away from celebrating. I think one of the reasons is that it smells very much like pride, and we want to steer clear of that stench. In an effort to avoid the accusation of "tooting our own horns," we usually move to the opposite end of the spectrum. But I encourage a celebration within the confines of humility. Such a celebration confirms the fact that a goal has been reached. There's absolutely nothing wrong with thanking God, and one another, for accomplishing what we've set out to do.

> Christian leaders often feel too busy to take the time to revel in the blessings God has handed out.

And if we don't pause to celebrate, we will wear out our helpers. In our volunteer-driven culture, an occasional attaboy and pat on the back go a long way toward attracting participation in the coming year. Several of our ministries have a yearly appreciation banquet for their volunteers in order to commend the volunteers for all they've accomplished. A mention in the church paper or from the pulpit also validates leadership and celebrates achievement.

Our Easter pageant is a big event. In preparation, nearly seven hundred actors, singers, instrumentalists, makeup artists, and technicians freely offer their gifts for a solid month. Their goal is for people to see Jesus Christ throughout every aspect of the program. Several years ago they realized something was missing: There was no party after the event. So now, a week later, after all these volunteers have caught up on their sleep and become reacquainted with their families, they hold a cast party. It lasts nearly three hours. Testimonies are shared, beards are shaved, and the room is filled with laughter and applause. In short, people *celebrate*.

For the past year I've been in an executive leadership–training program with twenty leaders of Christian organizations. We began our second meeting by recounting the biggest insights we took away from our first meeting together some five months earlier. Amazingly, a number of people recounted their conscious efforts to pause and celebrate their victories instead of immediately moving on to the next project. These efforts were prompted by a little reminder that was given to them at the end of our first meeting: Each was given an unused, deflated orange balloon to take back to his or her office. Now the orange balloons sit on their desks serving as a constant reminder to take the time to celebrate the victories.

Celebrate Leading Others to Christ

Jesus said, "I have come that they may have life, and have it to the full" (John 10:10). If you can't celebrate people placing their trust in Christ, then you've forgotten why you are in Christian leadership. Jesus gives us some insight into what happens in heaven when the lost are found: "I tell you, there is rejoicing in the presence of the angels of God over one sinner who repents" (Luke 15:10).

At our church, baptisms are usually held as a part of every worship service. Several years ago we ran into some awkward moments following these baptisms. Sometimes after one person was baptized, people would quietly affirm the decision, but at other times they would heartily applaud. And at other times, the baptism would be greeted with just a smattering of applause, which was a real downer.

The older folks of our church have gone through so much change (and handled it with such grace), that in deference to them we decided to make baptisms a time of reverence rather than celebration. We realized that some of the senior adults might be offended if we applauded during such a special moment in the service. Well, we gave it the old college try. The silence after baptisms lasted for a few weeks, and then the excitement was so great—from young and old alike—that people couldn't contain themselves. They spontaneously burst into applause. The congregation just wanted to celebrate, and rightfully so. Now we've reached a compromise: We've agreed that applause is fine, but we wait to applaud until the last person has emerged from the water.

> People couldn't contain themselves.

Recently, during a worship time, a song ended and the lights came up in the baptistery where one of our ministers was standing with his friend, Hall-of-Fame basketball coach, Denny Crum. When their images came up on the video screens, you could hear a murmur echoing through the crowd. But you could hear a pin drop as Denny Crum said, "I believe Jesus is the Christ, the Son of the living God, my Lord and Savior." When he came up out of the water, he was greeted with smiles, tears, and, as usual, applause.

If you listened intently, you probably heard more applause than usual. Is Denny Crum more important than anyone else who gets baptized? No. And he would be the first to tell you that. But because of his credibility and thirty-year coaching reputation in our city, people realized it took a lot of humility for him to don a white robe and wade into a small pool to admit his need for Jesus. That tells me Coach Crum wants to finish well, whether he has three more miles or just a hundred yards to go. In my mind that's cause for a celebration.

KEEPING YOUR HEAD ABOVE WATER

Preacher and author Max Lucado shared with me an idea he got when he spoke at an Amway convention a number of years ago. He said, "I've never seen such a celebration over the first-year people who had joined the Amway organization. I left thinking, *Why don't we do this within the church for new believers?* So now, each year on a Sunday called Dream Sunday, Max reads off the names of the people at Oak Hills Church of Christ who have been baptized during the previous year. These folks walk down the center aisle, where the elders stand and cheer for them along with the entire congregation.

What a great idea! With Max's blessing I adapted his idea to our setting. During the last week of the year, we held a Victory Weekend. In my sermon I invited hundreds who had become Christians during the year to come forward and fill the choir loft and seats on the side. The sight of hundreds of baptized believers walking down the center aisle amid choruses of praise provided a visual memory that won't soon be forgotten. Then I faced the new believers and challenged them to grow in Christ. It was truly a celebration. Max Lucado had the vision to create a "spiritual party" that was mutually beneficial to new believers as well as long-time Christians.

Celebrate "Leading Others to Lead"

As I write this book, Willow Creek Community Church is one of the largest churches in America. Pastor Bill Hybels says, "There's only one thing better than *casting* the vision, and that is *achieving* the vision." He knows that the vision can't be achieved if it isn't conveyed to and embraced by other leaders. We must pass the baton so that others may run the race. When they lead and minister effectively, we have all the more reason to celebrate.

For instance, I can celebrate Greg. About nine years ago, I went to lunch with him. In a recent sermon, he'd heard me challenge people to serve. He said, "I grew up playing baseball. A church our size should have some type of program where kids can play baseball, be mentored by Christians, and be challenged to live for the Lord." To make a long story short—we now have baseball!

Greg took it upon himself to lead this volunteer ministry. Team members and coaches pray before each game. The children work on a different memory verse throughout the week. They have a devotional time after the game. The emphasis is first upon Christ and then upon competition.

I hope you have some "Gregs" in your ministry. Three months out of the year, this soft-spoken servant spends his Friday nights and Saturdays pouring his life into hundreds of young people. He had a vision to use this league to attract kids (and their parents) to our church and to Christ. This year there are thirty-eight different teams (fourteen T-ball and twenty-four youth baseball teams).

For Greg, the celebration of his leadership doesn't come at the end of the season. His fulfillment comes each Saturday when he sees a child hit a ball for the first time or quote a Bible verse from memory. Greg's joy comes from parents who approach him and say, "We didn't go to church and didn't know the Lord. For two years our son played in this league and finally, one day, we went inside the church. Our lives have been totally changed through Christ. Thanks!"

Why save all of the celebration for the end of the trip? Enjoy the journey while you're on it, constantly celebrating those you are launching into leadership.

Celebrate the Privilege of Leading

Remember that at Rough River, before we started skiing, I stared at the back of the boat and verbalized my doubt: "Is that boat powerful enough to pull us up?" Since the other nine skiers had seen this boat pull ten people at once, they were aware of its power. I listened to my ski partners for the simple reason that they had experience and I didn't. They were convinced of the boat's power because they had witnessed it firsthand, and I followed them for that reason.

Joel Barker says, "A leader is someone I would follow to a place I am afraid to go by myself." The Holy Spirit leads by guiding and strengthening us in our weakness. When you first begin to serve the Lord, you may doubt what he can accomplish. But the longer you lead, the more confident you will become. If you've been leading for very long, then occasionally it is healthy to replay the highlight film of what the Spirit has accomplished through your ministry.

But please realize that this chapter is not about celebrating *your* accomplishments; it is about celebrating the *Lord's* accomplishments. When one of our leaders, Bob, is commended for his work, he's always appreciative but quick to focus the attention elsewhere. Sometimes he'll say, "If you see a turtle on a fence post you know he had some help getting there. That's how I feel about our church; God has grown it in spite of us."

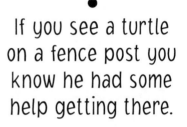

If you see a turtle on a fence post you know he had some help getting there.

If you are relying on the Spirit, your ministry can last longer than you think. God can "enlarge your territory" along with your ministry. Although you may retire and work fewer hours, understand this: The pace may change, but the passion must not. More can be celebrated as you let God's power work in you. Your age as a leader is secondary.

I love Ben Merold, who preaches at the Harvester Christian Church in St. Charles, Missouri. Ben built a church in southern California until its average attendance was over three thousand. At the age of sixty-five, he resigned and moved to Missouri, saying he would like to do it all over again. He took a church of three hundred and, in nine years' time, built it to over two thousand members.

When I spoke at a leadership seminar in St. Louis last year, guess who was sitting in the front row, listening intently and ferociously taking notes. That's right: Ben Merold. Ben succeeds in ministry because his effort and enthusiasm show that he's primarily a *learner* rather than a *knower*. Those who think they know it all may experience short-term success. Those who are lifelong learners continue to rise to the top because they're aware that the world they're trying to reach is constantly changing. That may explain why some Christian *knowers* limp into retirement in their early sixties while Christian *learners* are energized by realigning their ministries into other forms of service. Celebrations along the way validate their efforts and give these leaders their second wind.

When I was sixteen years old, I ran for president of my senior class. My body was going through some really weird changes. In my sophomore year I was 5'6", but by my junior year I was 6'1"! My trousers kept getting shorter and shorter. I can remember my parents trying to put off buying me pants until I stopped growing. That year, on more than one occasion, my dad said, "No, no, son. Your pants fit fine; knickers are coming back in style." It was an awkward time in my life, when my self-image was rather fragile. Like all teenagers, I wanted the approval and love of others. The significant risk and large dose of fear that accompany running for office didn't help.

> •
> Christian *learners* are energized by realigning their ministries into other forms of service.

The day of the speeches and voting was a long one for me. Just before the final bell, everyone at school was informed of the election results over the public address system. Do you know what I remember more vividly than the good news over the intercom? It was something that took place an hour later. I got off of the school bus and walked two blocks to my house. When I was about two hundred yards away, I saw a big poster on the front of our home, and I realized that my parents had made it. It said, "Win or lose—we love you!"

My parents didn't know the outcome of the election, but it didn't matter to them. In their minds, there was reason to celebrate regardless of the tally. *You tried, you finished, and that's what counts.* Even if my classmates didn't think I measured up, my parents wanted me to know that, in their eyes, I did.

God isn't consumed with your performance and success. He wants to celebrate the relationship you have with him, through the good times as well as the tough ones.

KEEPING YOUR HEAD ABOVE WATER

Yes, we can celebrate the privilege of leading, even as we experience the difficulties of leading. Years ago a group of ladies met regularly to study the Scriptures. While reading the third chapter of Malachi, they came upon a remarkable expression: "He will sit as a refiner and purifier of silver" (Malachi 3:3). As a result, one of the women decided to visit a silversmith to learn about the process of refining silver. After the silversmith had fully described the process to her, she asked, "Sir, what do you do while the work of refining is going on?"

"I must sit and watch the furnace constantly," he said. "For if the time necessary for refining is exceeded in the slightest degree, the silver will be damaged." The lady at once saw the beauty and comfort in the Scripture. "He will sit as a refiner and purifier of silver."

God may deem it necessary for his children to go into the furnace; but his eye is steadily intent on the work of purifying, and his wisdom and love for us are always engaged. Our trials are not randomly inflicted, and God will not let us be tested beyond our endurance. Before she left, the lady asked one final question: "How do you know when the process is complete?"

"That's quite simple," replied the silversmith. "When I can see my own image in the silver, the refining process is finished."

The Lord wants to see his image, not only in your life but also in your leadership. Allow him to refine you through the bad and good times. And then one day, when God looks at you and sees himself, it will be time to celebrate for eternity.

For Group Discussion

1. Which two or three paragraphs in this chapter are the most relevant to your situation? Why? Based on your experience, how might you state the thoughts in those paragraphs differently?

2. When have you most enjoyed celebrating a victory in your personal life? in your ministry?

3. How does your church celebrate conversions to Christ? baptisms? other victories in the life of the congregation?

4. Talk about a time you've successfully "led others to lead." What forms of celebration were (or could have been) appropriate?

5. Are you able to celebrate the privilege of ministry? How do you do it?

6. What, for you, are the "refining" aspects of your ministry? How do you maintain your sense of gratitude to God amid those trials?

●

CHAPTER nine

Looking Back, Looking Forward

I had done my best and made a memory that would last a lifetime.

Thank you for cruising along with me as we've analyzed the nature of leadership. Its lessons can be tough to learn, but leadership's particular satisfactions may be summed up in this phrase from the opening chapter: *I had done my best and made a memory that would last a lifetime.* That day at Rough River held a number of emotions: fear, excitement, exhilaration, fatigue, and joy—all part of the journey called leadership, all important parts of the process called change.

It's possible to read a book on leadership and applaud its message, but the true measure of its effectiveness is how it changes you. If you make no alterations to your leadership practices, then your time and money have been wasted. So my closing words in this chapter are meant to encourage you to put into practice what you've learned.

I'd like to suggest that the key to ongoing improvement can be found in looking in two directions: backward to reflect on the memories you've made and forward to envision your dreams coming to fruition.

Look Back and *Reflect*

The story line of this book evolved from a memorable experience. Making memories is a key task of a good leader. The more memories we make, the more lasting the impressions of the message we're proclaiming will be. So let me leave you with four things to keep in mind about memory making...

1. Be deliberate about the memories you make for yourself. Few memories spring from journeys that are never taken. If you're working with a group that refuses to begin a journey of growth, your only recourse is to lay the foundation for new leadership and gradually create memories as you go. Be on the lookout for opportunities to introduce positive changes, and when a chance does avail itself, don't hesitate—go for it.

Before we head off on a trip or begin a round of golf, my friend Mike occasionally says to me, "Let's go make a memory!" That is his way of saying, "There's no assurance that we'll ever get to do this again, so let's make it count." Those are good words for me to remember whether I'm playing golf, leading a meeting, or putting together a worship service.

Leadership is like a chain; each memory is another link in the chain. Regardless of how long you've been leading, deliberately make sure the journey is filled with memorable events that bring glory to God.

2. Inside the church, make memories so powerful that people absolutely have to see God. Plan events that are so excellent that only God could get the glory. Produce a memory that forces people, for maybe the first time in years, to pause and consider the gospel, all because the setting and the message came together in a way that powerfully reached their hearts.

When I'm out of town or on vacation and I miss one of our services at church, I call to see how things went. Invariably, the response is "You missed it—best sermon I've ever heard." When I respond that I'll buy the tape and listen to it, I'm usually told, "The tape doesn't do it justice. You had to be there!" These words convey an important idea: *Memories only come from experiences.* You have to be there!

Because I'm a preacher, I received the dubious honor of conducting the lakeside church service the evening of my water-skiing adventure. It's easy to remember things that are new, fresh, and out of the ordinary, so within a few hours of the adventure, I jotted down a page and a half of notes. My message that night centered around some parallels between the Christian life and the adventure on the lake I had experienced just a few hours earlier.

One of my close friends once preached a sermon on repentance and forgiveness that was new, fresh, and out of the ordinary, especially in its conclusion. He invited the worshippers to write their struggles on a piece of paper with the heading "God, please forgive me for..." (Participants then listed the sins by which Satan had held them hostage.) At the end of the service,

> A dramatic experience can drive home the point of a sermon as nothing else can.

the participants walked forward and placed their written prayers in a big basket at the foot of the cross. The collected cards were then burned. At first they smoldered, and then there was a small explosion. Rick said, "That must have been mine!" But I'll bet everybody felt that way.

No one will forget that service. A dramatic experience can drive home the point of a sermon as nothing else can. (Such events must be occasional rather than typical; if you burn your sins up each week, then everyone will lose interest—except, of course, the fire marshal.)

3. Outside the church, make memories that are both excellent and relevant. Leaders need to recognize what resonates with those outside the walls of their church buildings. Have you noticed that, in our society today, the simple activities of everyday life have been transformed into personalized memory makers? My friend John told of receiving a pair of Nike shoes as a gift from his son. John said, "I was instructed to go to the Web site to choose the exact colors I preferred. Later I was mailed a Nike T-shirt. Nike personalized my shoes by putting my name on them and even mailed me a document that I could frame."

Why go to so much trouble for something that people put on their feet? The marketing folks at Nike realize that people like memorable events. What a message for Christian leaders who want to influence the world!

How else can you explain why intelligent people walk into Starbucks and spend $4 on a cup of coffee that costs only a quarter to make? People are in search of an experience, and they are willing to pay top dollar for it. Starbucks offers outlets for their customers' laptop computers. Starbucks creates a setting for meeting new people and conversing with old friends. The aroma of the coffee activates the sense of smell, adding to the memory. In fact, Starbucks reaches all the senses, making drinking coffee with friends an event to be remembered rather than a routine to be endured. (Hello, Christian leaders! Are you listening?)

Now I'm not advocating making worship into a Tinseltown production. In fact, inappropriate bells and whistles too often achieve the opposite of the intended effect. I've seen Christian leaders continually try to top the special effects of the previous week until the whole enterprise loses its sense of purpose. Worship that is effective and memorable doesn't require special effects; it just needs to be excellent and absolutely relevant.

4. Always remember the power of spiritual experience over spiritual speech. This is how Leonard Sweet, dean of the theological school at Drew University, puts it: "Churches in postmodern communities will be built, not around great preachers, but around great experiences."[1]

Ouch! While that statement may sting us preachers, it rings of the truth, doesn't it? Are you creating memories or just having meetings? It's time the church realized that it is impossible to reach a compact-disc culture with 8-track methodology. Memory-maker events include small impressions that last a week and big events that last a lifetime. But remember, memories are not an end in themselves. They must be accompanied by sound biblical teaching. The memorable experience grabs people; the Word of God keeps them. So what's the water-skiing experience in your life to which the people in your ministry can relate? Learn from it and share it.

> **The memorable experience grabs people; the Word of God keeps them.**

Look Forward and *Dream*

It's not enough to merely look back. Someone has said, "The only thing that makes the good old days, the good old days, is a poor memory!" I was plotting the next ski event before I had even dried off because that's the way God wired me. My mind raced to devise a way to have eleven skiers participate next year.

We need time to let ideas bubble up from our souls or flow down to us from heaven. We need time to sit with our ideas and let them take shape according to God's will and timing. We simply need time to consider the future with God. So I invite you to set aside moments in your days for these three critical tasks related to your future...

1. Pray—and "act like" the future. Remember to plan some Focus Days so you can dream of how God might deepen your leadership. Take the time to pray about how God can use you in the future, then act the part.

What do I mean by that? Consider the approach of Dr. David Yonggi Cho, pastor of the Yoido Full Gospel Church in Seoul, South Korea. About twenty years ago, I heard Pastor Cho speak at a church in southern Indiana. At the time, his church was only a fledgling congregation of a paltry two hundred thousand! Yet his church-growth principles seemed a little bizarre to this twenty-one-year-old.

Pastor Cho said, "When my church was averaging five hundred in attendance, I wanted to be a preacher of a church of one thousand. So I began to walk around and act like I was a preacher of a church of one thousand. Soon, I was. So then I began to walk like I was the preacher of a church of five thousand. Soon, I was."

On and on he went. Everyone clapped and laughed as he progressed through the growth spurts of his congregation. (When I went back to my church and tried the "walking thing," all I got was a sore back!)

As you observe the experience of Pastor Cho and his church, you begin to see that aside from "his walk," the real secret was his prayer. Gimmicks don't work when it comes to vision casting. What does work is to dream big and to persevere through the small, seemingly insignificant steps toward the goal. That is when God rewards your faithfulness and gives you the desires of your heart.

Solomon stated, "Where there is no vision the people perish" (Proverbs 29:18). God has plans for you. He makes this quite clear in Jeremiah 29:11: " 'For I know the plans I have for you,' declares the Lord, 'plans to prosper you and not to harm you, plans to give you hope and a future.' "

Pray for his plans to come to pass. And act as if he is going to keep his promise.

2. Release your sanctified imagination! What are your dreams for the advancement of the gospel? Might God have some big plans for you? Just imagine what he could do!

"No eye has seen, no ear has heard, no mind has conceived what God has prepared for those who love him" (1 Corinthians 2:9).

In October of 2000 I had the privilege of performing the wedding ceremony of Steve Henry and Heather Renee French. At the time, Steve was the lieutenant governor of the state of Kentucky and, two weeks before this, Heather had completed her reign as Miss America 2000. As you can imagine, the wedding attracted a great deal of attention. It was held in a beautiful downtown cathedral, and the service was beamed throughout the state on live television.

KEEPING YOUR HEAD ABOVE WATER

Steve and Heather committed to allowing the Lord to be at the center of their marriage. As Miss America, Heather chose as her "platform" to speak up for a group of people who don't have much of a voice—homeless veterans. It was amazing to see the encouragement she brought to such an important yet forgotten group.

When people ask me what the highlight of the weekend was, they are sometimes taken aback by my reply. To me, it was the rehearsal dinner—a time away from the cameras and lights. About sixty people enjoyed a meal at a nice restaurant in a private room. After the meal, Steve's buddies stood up, one by one, and mercilessly chided him. Then some of Heather's friends shared their good wishes.

But just when I thought it was time to go home, Heather's older brother, Jeremy, stood up and started talking. He walked over and stood behind Heather and placed his hands on her shoulders. Instantly something happened. This young woman, a picture of poise and beauty, began to cry. Tears streamed down her cheeks while she listened to Jeremy share from his heart. This is what I recall him saying:

> God wants to use the part of your self that dreams dreams and generates possibilities.

"When we were growing up, people would always ask us kids, 'What are you going to do?' or 'What are you going to be when you grow up?'

"And as a little girl, Heather was always saying, 'I'm going to make a difference in this world. I'm going to make a difference in this world.'

"In my mind I thought, *Yeah, right. How could one girl from Maysville, Kentucky, make a difference?*

"But I've watched her this year, and I have seen Heather do just that. I've kind of plateaued in my goal setting; she hasn't. Now she inspires me to want to make a difference too."

I believe Heather's brother went home to do some powerful imagining that night about what God could do in his life during the years to come. So...when have you done the same? God wants to use the part of your self that dreams dreams and generates possibilities. He will apply his almighty power to your deepest desires to please him. Imagine what could result.

3. Start something that only God can finish. Steve
Reeves tells the story of a woman who underwent a very delicate form of brain surgery. In removing the tumor, the doctors were concerned that the slightest miscue could cause the loss of either her memory or her eyesight. So they asked the woman to choose which side of the brain tissue they'd enter with their scalpels. In other words, if she had to lose one of those senses, which would she prefer to lose? Wisely, she said, "Let me think about it overnight, and I'll tell you tomorrow which sense is more important to me."

The next day she told the doctors, "If I had to lose either memory or sight, I would prefer to lose my memory."

When asked how she arrived at her decision, she calmly replied, "I'd rather see where I'm going than remember where I've been."

Memories are important, but God is more concerned with where you are leading than where you've been. How about it? Do you ever dream of making a difference in this world? Are you willing to trust God to make those dreams come true? Dr. Bob Pierce says, "Most people never see a miracle because they never tackle anything that *requires* a miracle. God doesn't waste his miracles."

A Christian leader who inspires and leads others can make a huge difference to a world in search of Christ. You don't have to look like Heather Henry or walk like Pastor Cho. You just need to make some memories, cast the vision, and allow the Lord to lead *you*! When he calls you to begin the task, have no fear—he will see that it is completed. Then you won't be worrying about *keeping your head above water*; your leadership will be blessed and lives will be changed for eternity.

"Being confident of this,
that he who began a good work in you
will carry it on to completion
until the day of Christ Jesus"
(Philippians 1:6).

For Group Discussion

1. What are your best memories of church as a child? as an adult?

2. What makes for good memories in ministry? Can you share an example from your own experience?

3. Why does spiritual *experience* often have a more powerful impact than spiritual *speech*? What are some implications of this for your ministry?

4. Are you comfortable with the idea of a "sanctified imagination"? What does this mean for you, personally?

5. When have you started something that only God could finish? Tell what happened!

NOTES

Chapter 2

1. John C. Maxwell, *Leadership 101—Inspirational Quotes & Insights for Leaders* (Tulsa, OK: Honor Books, 1997), 5.

2. Charles R. Swindoll, *The Birth of an Exciting Vision* (Anaheim, CA: Insight for Living, 1992), 135.

3. Philip Yancey, *The Jesus I Never Knew* (Grand Rapids, MI: Zondervan, 1995), 99-100.

Chapter 3

1. Richard A. Swenson, M.D., *The Overload Syndrome* (Colorado Springs, CO: NavPress, 1999), 123-125.

2. Max Lucado, quoted in Christian Standard (September 3, 1996), 3.

3. John Ortberg, *The Life You've Always Wanted* (Grand Rapids, MI: Zondervan, 1997), 83.

Chapter 4

1. C.S. Lewis, *The Screwtape Letters* (New York: Macmillan Publishing Company, 1961), 33.

2. Olan Hendrix, CMA Management Monthly, (May, 2000, No. 42), 2.

3. Chuck Swindoll, *Intimacy with the Almighty* (Nashville, TN: J. Countryman, 1999). 38.

4. Stephen R. Covey, A. Roger Merrill, and Rebecca R. Merrill, *First Things First* (New York: Simon & Schuster, 1994), 19.

Chapter 5

1. Henry Hoenig, Louisville magazine (October, 1998), 47.

2. Angela Thomas Guffey, Focus on the Family magazine (May, 2001), 8.

Chapter 6

1. John Maxwell, *Leadership 101—Inspirational Quotes & Insights for Leaders* (Tulsa, OK: Honor Books, 1997), 69.

2. Russell H. Ewing, quoted in "Notes, Thoughts & Ideas on Trends and Issues in Leadership & Philanthropy," The Covenant Group (April/May, 2001), 2.

3. Dave Stone, *I'd Rather See a Sermon* (Joplin, MO: College Press Publishing Co., 1996), 117.

4. Walter Wriston, quoted in *Developing the Leaders Around You* by John C. Maxwell (Nashville, TN: Thomas Nelson, Inc., 1995), 151-152.

Chapter 7

1. John Bradley and Jay Carty, *Unlocking Your Sixth Suitcase* (Colorado Springs, CO: NavPress), 131.

2. John D. Beckett, *Loving Monday* (Downers Grove, IL: InterVarsity Press, 1998), 162.

3. Survey reported in New Man magazine (May/June, 2001), 25.

4. Henri Nouwen, *In the Name of Jesus* (New York: Crossroad Publishing, 1989), 47-48.

5. George MacDonald, quoted in *Maranatha! The NIV Worship Bible* (Grand Rapids, MI: Zondervan, 2000), 1604.

Chapter 9

1. Leonard Sweet, *SoulTsunami* (Grand Rapids, MI: Zondervan, 1999), 199.

Suggested Reading

Blanchard, Ken, et al. *Leadership by the Book: Tools to Transform Your Workplace*. New York: William Morrow and Company, Inc., 1999.

Blanchard, Kenneth H. and Spencer Johnson. *The One Minute Manager*. New York: Berkley Publishing Group, 1983.

De Pree, Max. *Leadership Is an Art*. New York: Dell Publishing Company, Inc., 1990.

Hutchens, David. *Outlearning the Wolves: Surviving and Thriving in a Learning Organization*. Waltham, MA: Pegasus Communications, Inc., 1998.

Johnson, Spencer. *Who Moved My Cheese?* New York: The Putnam Publishing Group, 1998.

Maxwell, John C. *The 21 Irrefutable Laws of Leadership*. Nashville: Thomas Nelson, 1998.

von Oech, Robert. *A Whack on the Side of the Head: How You Can Be More Creative*. New York: Time Warner, 1998.

Russell, Bob with Rusty Russell. *When God Builds a Church: 10 Principles for Growing a Dynamic Church*. West Monroe, LA: Howard Publishing Company, 2000.

Stone, Sam E. *How to Be an Effective Church Leader*. Joplin, MO: College Press, 2001.

Sweet, Leonard. *AquaChurch*. Loveland, CO: Group Publishing, Inc., 1999.

Sweet, Leonard. *Soul Tsunami: Sink or Swim in New Millennium Culture*. Grand Rapids, MI: Zondervan Publishing House, 1999.

Taylor, Barbara Brown. *When God Is Silent*. Boston: Cowley Publications, 1998.

KEEPING YOUR HEAD ABOVE WATER

Group Publishing, Inc.
Attention: Product Development
P.O. Box 481
Loveland, CO 80539
Fax: (970) 679-4370

Evaluation for
Keeping Your Head Above Water

Please help Group Publishing, Inc. continue to provide innovative and useful resources for ministry. Please take a moment to fill out this evaluation and mail or fax it to us. Thanks!

● ● ●

1. As a whole, this book has been (circle one)
not very helpful   very helpful

| 1 | 2 | 3 | 4 | 5 | 6 | 7 | 8 | 9 | 10 |

2. The best things about this book:

3. Ways this book could be improved:

4. Things I will change because of this book:

5. Other books I'd like to see Group publish in the future:

6. Would you be interested in field-testing future Group products and giving us your feedback? If so, please fill in the information below:

name _____

Church name_____

Denomination _____ Church Size_____

Church Address _____

City _____ State _____ ZIP_____

Church Phone _____

E-mail _____

Exciting Resources for Your Adult Ministry!

The Dirt on Learning

Thom & Joani Schultz

This thought-provoking book explores what Jesus' Parable of the Sower says about effective teaching *and* learning. Readers will rethink the Christian education methods used in their churches and consider what really works. Use the video training kit to challenge and inspire your entire ministry team and set a practical course of action for Christian education methods that really *work*!

Book Only	ISBN 0-7644-2088-7
Video Training Kit	ISBN 0-7644-2152-2

The Family-Friendly Church

Ben Freudenburg with Rick Lawrence

Discover how certain programming can often short-circuit your church's ability to truly strengthen families—and what you can do about it! You'll get practical ideas and suggestions featuring profiles of real churches. It also includes thought-provoking application worksheets that will help you apply the principles and insights to your own church.

ISBN 0-7644-2048-8

Disciple-Making Teachers

Josh Hunt with Dr. Larry Mays

This clear, practical guide equips teachers of adult classes to have impact—and produce disciples eager for spiritual growth and ministry. You get a Bible-based, proven process that's achieved results in churches like yours—and comes highly recommended by Christian leaders like Dr. Bruce Wilkinson, Findley Edge, and Robert Coleman. Discover what needs to happen before class through preparation, in class during teaching, and after class in service to turn your adult classes into disciple groups.

ISBN 0-7644-2031-3

Extraordinary Results From Ordinary Teachers

Michael D. Warden

Now both professional *and* volunteer Christian educators can teach as Jesus taught! You'll explore the teaching style and methods of Jesus and get clear and informed ways to deepen your teaching and increase your impact! This is an essential resource for every teacher, youth worker, or pastor.

ISBN 0-7644-2013-5

Discover our full line of children's, youth, and adult ministry resources at your local Christian bookstore, or write: Group Publishing, P.O. Box 485, Loveland, CO 80539. www.grouppublishing.com